PERSONAL POLITICAL POWER

IN CALIFORNIA

How to Take Action & Make a Difference

JOEL BLACKWELL
THE GRASSROOTS GUY

Advocacy Publishing
SACRAMENTO, CALIFORNIA

Advocacy Publishing
1017 L Street #472
Sacramento CA 95814-3805
www.JoelBlackwell.com
GrassRootsGuy@JoelBlackwell.com
916.277.4884

Ordering Information:
Quantity sales. Special discounts are available on quantity purchases by corporations, associations, and others. For details, contact the "Special Sales Department" at the address above.

Personal Political Power in California/Joel Blackwell—1st ed.
ISBN 978-0-9669236-3-6
Library of Congress Control Number: 2015932197

"We in America do not have government by the majority. We have government by the majority who participate."

—Thomas Jefferson

A REFLECTION

As I was closing a seminar in Washington, a woman stood up to get my attention, very agitated. I thought she was angry. "Joel," she shouted, "you left something out." She went on to explain that she had been in my seminar the year before and I said something that changed her life.

"You told us last year that the people who write the letters, write the laws. I took it to heart and went home and started writing letters and it's true.

They pay attention."

Honestly, I did not remember saying that, although I have many times since.

TABLE OF CONTENTS

PART II: The People

PART III: The Tools

About This Book

This book is in three main parts:

Part I: The Process Fourteen chapters full of tips and techniques for how to assert your personal political power to get what you want with California legislators.

Part II: The Tools Three appendices full of charts, checklists and sample written communications.

Part III: The People Commentary from political figures about how they deal with people who want something from them.

You will learn how to operate effectively as an influencer of public policy, and you will be among a group of people that comprise less than one percent of all Americans.

I invite you to first read it all the way through, and then go back and see what steps you want to take to be able to work effectively with politicians to get what you want.

PART I

The Process

CHAPTER ONE

How You Can Harness the Most Powerful Moment in Politics

That moment is when a voter talks to an elected official they can vote for. You will learn how to communicate and get action from elected officials; how to work through an organization and get results on legislative issues. I will show you that you can have significant influence without ever looking at that chart "How a bill moves through the legislature" and without spending a lot of time and money. If you get engaged as I suggest, you will meet interesting people, have fun and make a difference.

Although the techniques here will work anywhere, this book focuses on California. That means how to get the action you want on bills in the Assembly and Senate in Sacramento. I also include references to members of Congress because California is an important state for federal issues. If you live here, you have the opportunity to influence national policy.

Please understand, this book is about legislators and legislation, not what people in politics call "case work." That is a personal problem that affects only you, such as your dispute with an insurance company or a missing payment from the state. If you are trying to resolve some issue like that and your elected official can help, they will.

That's their job and politicians and their staff are happy to help —if they can —because they know every successful case turns into votes.

Issues and policy, on the other hand, are things that will be decided in the California Senate and Assembly. My goal is to help you achieve your goal and get what you want from those two legislative bodies. I don't care about your political identity, party or issue. I believe in democracy. You achieve your goals by winning the support of enough senators and assembly members at each step of what is likely to be a long and convoluted process. Don't be discouraged, though. A constant theme through this book is that our system works— for those who work it. You, your issue and your organization can win.

I emphasize "organization" because of one key operating principle: Don't expect politicians to pay attention to you if you represent just one person with a good idea for a policy or law. They don't have time to devote to such matters because there are too many equally good ideas that have widespread support from broad-based organizations called special interest groups.

Am I saying you probably won't get much unless you are part of a special interest group? Yes, and it's important to understand why. For starters, the U.S. Constitution supports and enables special interest groups. Such groups are a key element in finding and expressing consensus.

Despite this, you will often hear politicians deriding the power of "special interest groups." This is balderdash for the consumption of uninformed, disengaged masses and the people spouting this nonsense know it. The newspapers and television routinely portray "special interest groups" as a version of the AIDS virus, a plague upon the Republic that needs to be eradicated. I hope that when you've finished this book, you will have a different view.

Next time you hear a politician railing against "special interest groups," ask them: "Which special interest groups have too much power? Teachers? Bankers? School boards? Realtors? Boy Scouts? Catholic Church? Insurance agents? What would you do to curtail their power? Fact is, any honest politician will tell you that the government, and certainly the politicians, couldn't function without special interest lobbying groups and their volunteer and professional staff.

Here's one analysis:

"Lobbyists are, in many cases, expert technicians and capable of explaining complex and difficult subjects in a clear, understandable fashion. They engage in personal discussions with Members of Congress in which they can explain in detail the reasons for positions they advocate.... Because our congressional representation is based on geographical boundaries, the lobbyists who speak for the various economic, commercial and other functional interests of this country serve a very useful purpose and have assumed an important role in the legislative process." —Senator JOHN KENNEDY, Congressional Record, March 2, 1956, vol. 102, pp. 3802–3

If you want to change law or policy in any political arena—city, county, state or the United States—you need to show broad-based support. You do that by joining or forming a special interest group and mobilizing people who can vote for the politicians who can give you what you want. That's all a special interest group is: like-minded people joining together to fight for a cause. Having an organization is important because if you are the only person who wants something, why should your needs define public policy?

That's why we have a system in which special interest groups play a huge role: Special interest groups demonstrate depth of support beyond one person. After all, "majority rule" means you have and can show a majority. If you don't like our political system—the way money works, the way special interest groups work—I encourage you to try to change it. This book will help. On some structural issues, such as the role of money, many politicians and lobbyists will agree with you. I probably agree with you. But I don't see the system changing anytime soon. For now, I'm trying to help you get what you want from the system as it exists, using tried and proven techniques. Everything that follows assumes you can work through an organization.

Basic Concepts You Need to Understand

Our political system is not designed to decide, and cannot decide, who is right and who is wrong. It is designed to decide who has a majority.

- ✓ There are no right or wrong positions in politics, just decisions made by human beings for good reasons, bad reasons or indifference.
- ✓ If you can't prove that lots of people are with you, you will fail.
- ✓ If you have the votes in the legislature, you're right. If you don't, you're wrong.
- ✓ No political decision is permanent; the fat lady never sings.

CHAPTER TWO

A Little Background

My political education began when I ran for a seat in the North Carolina House of Representatives many years ago. I came to understand the most important dynamic in politics: The special relationship between politicians and the people who put them in office—the voters in their district.

This realization came as I shook hands and talked with voters. I was both very interested in what they had to say and how I could get their votes. Later I spoke with politicians and lobbyists and explored the vast research into how politicians make decisions. I learned a lot about how politicians feel about the people who can vote for them and how powerful those people can be.

Elected officials lust for voter approval. Constituents are the most important people in the world, and every candidate or elected official must pay attention to them. They are like customers, and if they don't buy what you are selling, you will be out of office. Elected officials know they must listen to the people who can vote for them, or else.

You see this principal hammered home time and again, most recently in Virginia. The Majority Leader of the U.S. House of Representatives, Eric Cantor, was described by *The New York Times* as spending so much time on national party politics that "he was leaving the home fires dangerously unattended." He got beat in a primary. A smart politician never forgets who put him in office and who can take him out: the voters back home.

I spent a lot of time shaking hands and talking with voters. Now, my personal goal is to get every concerned American to speak, as a representative or member of an organized group, to the people they vote for, just as the writers of the Constitution intended. If we do that, we can solve every problem the nation faces.

But Americans are sinking into cynicism and doubt about our political system. Almost everything you see on TV or read in the newspaper feeds that cynical point of view. The presentation of politics in newspapers, on television and online feeds negativity and gives people an easy excuse to shun political activity. To an outsider, it all seems about money, power, and sometimes sex. That is not the reality I have experienced. Our system is not perfect by any stretch of the imagination, but it works for those who work it. Make a note: FOR THOSE WHO WORK IT. People aren't left out; they drop out.

We all know how few people take even the simplest step to participate in our political system: vote. In most elections, such as Assembly races here in California, only 20 percent to 40 percent of eligible people vote. An even smaller number make meaningful contact with an elected officeholder about an issue. My grassroots poll found that about 13 percent of Americans have contributed money or time to a politician.

Other polls found even fewer, depending on how the question is asked.

In the June 2014 California primary, only 25 percent of California registered voters cast a ballot, 4.4 million out of 17.7 million registered—about half the population of Los Angeles County. Los Angeles, because of its population and the number of legislators it sends to Sacramento, is a major center of political clout. Even so, it consistently has the lowest turnout rate of any county in the state, a mere 17 percent in 2014. (Voting is important. Please vote, although later I will discuss why voting is the least effective means to affect public policy.)

That so few people vote, that far fewer write to or make phone calls to politicians, and almost none give money or time means that those who do communicate wield disproportionate power. People who write letters, send emails, make contributions and phone calls, or give time to politicians form a small political elite that drives public policy.

My experience, and that of many other political professionals, tells me fewer than one percent of Americans communicate often enough and effectively enough to influence policy. You can be in that one percent, the political elite.

It amazes me, as I work with ordinary people from San Diego to Boston to Miami, that those who get involved get results. They don't always get everything they want—nobody does—but they believe there is a fair process and they often win something.

Contrary to the image presented in newspapers and on TV, nearly all of those people who talk to politicians and work with them will tell you that elected officeholders are honest, hardworking men and women of high ethical standards who are trying their best to find satisfactory compromises to complicated problems.

However, many people fall into the trap of believing that the corruption and failures reported in the media represent all politicians. If you are in that group, just note that what you are seeing are the people who got caught. This proves the system works. If you respond by saying, well, there are plenty who don't get caught, I disagree. Nobody is watched more than elected officials. It is difficult to do anything without the whole world finding out. My experience and gut feeling is that politicians are more honest than most people if for no other reason than it is so difficult for them to escape scrutiny. It is true that many politicians operate within the cycle of taking campaign contributions, then helping those contributors achieve their goals, then getting more contributions. That's legal and doesn't mean they were bought. It's a symbiotic relationship. Note that the campaign contributions DO NOT go to the candidate but to their campaign, an important distinction.

I also believe—and this is based on conversations with hundreds of staff, politicians and lobbyists—that most people run for office out of a sincere desire to do good, as they define "good."

Whether you believe that or not, I can promise you that adopting a positive attitude is the first step toward getting what you want. Maintaining a negative attitude will do nothing but hurt you.

I hope this book will energize you to understand the constitutional role of special interest groups, become engaged and make this democracy work as it should. We don't have political parties that engage citizens to pass legislation. As the founders intended, our system has evolved into a special interest democracy. One of my favorite type of clients over the years has been Realtors®. They are fond of saying, "We're not Democrats; we're not Republicans. We are the Realtor Party."

We Americans form and express consensus through organizations, not political parties. That's how advocates gather the critical mass of political weight needed to move Congress or the California legislature. It's very important to understand this. When you read in the newspapers or see on TV that the "Democratic Party" or the "Republican Party" has done something in Congress or the legislature, it's misleading. A better description would be, "the Democratic caucus" or "House Republicans." To call movers and shakers a "party" invokes an image of citizen participation that simply doesn't exist. Citizens don't enact legislation through parties but through special interest groups. If you doubt this, go down to any political party office three months after an election, if you can find one. Try to "join" the party to advocate for your issue. Let me know what happens.

I've worked in 47 states teaching people how to lobby. In my seminars I say, "All things being equal, politicians will go with the flow. Your job is to create the flow." You can do that if you represent a consensus rather than a single individual. Usually this means an organization of the sort envisioned in the First Amendment: special interest groups contributing to public discourse already up and running and in the fight. Your best bet is to join a group and leverage your effort.

CHAPTER THREE

How to Get
What You Want

First, start with the magic numbers. In Congress, for any bill that matters, it takes 60 votes in the U.S. Senate and 218 in the House to pass. After that, you need the support of the President and then you have to work with the bureaucrats or regulators who write the rules. Those people can give you what you want. It's sort of like being in school. You can get 90s and A's or you can get 70s and C's, but you still pass and graduate. Anything less than 70 and you fail. When you add 218 in the House and 60 in the Senate, you pass. You win. Anything else is gravy. (If you face a presidential veto, to override it will take a two-thirds vote in both houses: 67 in the senate and 290 in the house. Good luck!) Those are the magic numbers at the federal level.

In the California legislature, it usually takes 41 of 80 assembly members and 21 of 40 senators to create the magic number. For most issues, you can succeed with far fewer, but with those numbers, and the governor on your side, it's hard to lose. So, how do you get to the magic numbers?

Here Are the Four Essential Tools You Need

1. Professional lobbying staff. You need someone on the inside who understands the system and who will focus on your issues 24/7/365. A volunteer cannot devote the necessary time and can't possibly know enough. Professional staff should help you develop a list of target politicians (who can give you what you want), develop an inside strategy, and tell you what to do and when to do it. The "inside" strategy is the plan to get votes in committee and onto the floor, and to get a bill passed or stopped. The "outside" strategy includes how to use money, media and grassroots advocates in the district to persuade those politicians to vote with you.

2. Money. Anybody who is determined and has something rational to say can get a politician to listen. But, just like everyone else, politicians listen best and pay the most attention to people they know and like, and who have been supportive. Money demonstrates support. Money is an important tool, but don't make the mistake of thinking you get a vote for giving legal money. It's also true that plenty of groups win without money. A core idea in this book is that good grass roots organizing can overcome a lack of money and combat those who have money.

3. Media. Newspapers set the political agenda in their circulation area, even in this era of Facebook, Twitter and bloggers. Television doesn't. The Internet doesn't. If a newspaper says an issue is important with coverage and editorials, then politicians (and television and the Internet) will pay attention. Using media to amplify and deliver your message can be a powerful tool. Getting coverage on the editorial pages and in the news pages and on TV can get the attention of politicians whose help you need. Despite the hue and cry, I don't see bloggers and other Internet media impacting politicians to vote one way or another on legislation. But the impact of the Internet is growing and it might be that individual politicians come under much greater scrutiny on a day-to-day basis through the 'net.

4. Members. As a participant in your advocacy organization, your job is to communicate a specific message to the politician in whose district you work or vote. You must convince them that (1) a lot of people (2) in the district (3) whom the politician needs (4) care about the issue and (5) care a lot. You accomplish this by describing how the issue affects your life, your work and you, and by getting others to do the same in a thoughtful, personal manner.

You have enormous power when you tell your personal story, the story of your job, your life and the other people who can vote for the person you are talking to. It's almost as strong even if you don't physically live in the district, but work in the district. ("District" refers to the area represented by U.S. House members, and members of state legislatures. The "district" for U.S. Senators is their state.)

If you work, live or vote in a politician's district, they care about you. You have valuable information. I have talked with hundreds of elected officials from the U.S. Senate down to mayors and city council members. Again and again they say that they need people like you to help them understand how policy plays out in practice. What is the impact on the street? On your family, employer, friends and neighbors? For your issue, you are an expert because you live and breathe it every day.

When you realize you only have to talk about the subjects you already know, it makes your job easier. You don't have to be an expert on parliamentary procedure, the committee system, or anything else. You do not need to know how a bill moves through the legislature, although that is useful. Just tell your story about your issue.

For your issue, you know more than the elected officials. You probably know more than the professional lobbyist. Your elected officials want to benefit from your knowledge and experience. You can also make the story come alive with personal experiences and specific stories that put a face on the issue and make it memorable.

Your ability to win in the California legislature turns more on your ability to make the issue come alive with true stories than any other single factor. Every time I ask a politician to give an example of being influenced, they tell about someone who put a face on the issue with a personal anecdote. Like soap opera fans, they love a good story.

What is Grass Roots Politics?

If you search the Internet for "grassroots" or "grass roots," you will get a lot of lawn companies, florists and political organizations of all kinds.

"Grassroots" in a political sense means organized at the most basic level—individual people. Rudyard Kipling used "grass roots" in his 1901 novel *Kim* to mean the origin or source ("Not till I came to Shamlegh could I meditate upon the Course of Things, or trace the running grass-roots of Evil.").

In the United States, the first use of the word "grassroots" in a political sense is usually attributed to Senator Albert Jeremiah Beveridge of Indiana. He said of the Progressive Party in 1912 that "This party has come from the grass roots. It has grown from the soil of people's hard necessities."

I use the term to describe the most powerful moment in politics: constituents talking, writing, phoning and meeting with the person for whom they can vote.

CHAPTER FOUR

The Voting Contradiction

Some will argue that the real source of political power, for most people, is their right to vote. Certainly after the disputed and close Presidential elections of 2000, 2004 and 2008, we know voting is important. I urge my clients to get their people registered. It's the entry-level act to achieve political clout. It's important and I hope you will vote. I emphasize this because what I say next is hard for people to understand, and I want you to know that I believe in voting.

Voting is the least influential weapon in your political arsenal. It makes a difference by default. Bad things may happen if you don't vote. Voting seldom makes good things happen.

Of all actions, voting is least likely to enable you to affect policy or legislation.

Voting is the most difficult and costly weapon to mobilize.

You can only vote every two, four, or six years depending on the office.

You can only vote for a few people. They may not be the ones who determine your fate. Your own member of Congress or the legislature may not be in a position to help you because he or she isn't in leadership (those who control the House and Senate, the governor and the president) or because they just don't have the clout.

Your vote only determines who gets elected, if that, and only affects the district in which you live.

Even if your candidate wins, you haven't told them what to do and they may not agree with you on your issue.

I know, just a few votes more in Florida and Al Gore would have been president. Just a few more in Ohio and John Kerry would have been president.

Sometimes it's close and every vote really counts. Governor Christine Gregoire of Washington State was elected in 2004 by 129 votes out of 2.6 million cast. After the state supreme court ruled that "one or more" votes were invalid in a Montana race, the Democrats gained control of the State House of Representatives. The 2006 U.S. Senate race in Virginia was very close and determined which party would be in control of the U.S. Senate. Cathleen Galgiani won a seat in the California Senate in 2012 by less than 7,000 votes out of 281,927 cast, a 1 percent squeaker. In the 2014 statewide California primary to decide the top two candidates for controller who would be on the ballot in November, No. 2 won by 481 votes out of 4,039,375. Sometimes just a few votes matter. I always vote, and I hope you will.

But in fact, outcomes of district and state elections are rarely in doubt and the close races cited here are exceptional and rare.

Even so, remember that in 2006, 93 percent of House seats did not change party hands. In the Senate it was 94 percent. Put another way, the incumbent or the incumbent's party was returned to office in 432 of 468 races (435 in the House and 33 in the Senate).

In 2012 there were 63 U.S. House seats where the margin of victory was less than 10 percent. That was a presidential year of high political interest.

Since 1996 more than 98 percent of incumbents in Congress have been re-elected and it's about the same in California assembly elections except for those who are term-limited out of office. Here is a key to success in achieving your legislative goals: 95+ percent of people in office will stay in office as long as they want and legally can and there is nothing you can do about it. Even if you back a candidate who wins, your person may never have significant influence and may never be a player in the issues that are important to you.

Despite all of that, please vote. In a rare instance, your vote might determine who gets elected. But in the case of most issues that touch you, you have little or no power to make change through elections and it doesn't matter who is elected. Here's why:

1. In California general elections, the candidate must receive a plurality and the winner takes all. Only candidates who run as "plain vanilla" can win. A smart candidate sits squarely in the middle of the road—as "middle" is defined in the election district—and takes as few stands as possible on as few issues as possible. They have to. Every time a candidate takes a stand, they are more likely to arouse opposition than supporters. So most issues never come up in an election in any meaningful way.

2. Issues raised in elections tend to be the popular, lightning rod issues, often social issues. Crime, abortion, welfare, education, the economy, the death penalty, immigration, social security, health care, gas prices. Most of these issues are so intractable that nobody can do much more than make a marginal change, no matter what. However, they are all great campaign issues. They arouse passion in the electorate and generate votes. They are important. But what, realistically, can anyone do about them? The issues discussed in most campaigns, and the issues candidates tend to promote, have little or nothing to do with you anyway. Your issue probably won't come up in a campaign and the candidates probably will not be aware of it.

Of the issues that members of Congress and state legislatures work on, 99.44 percent are never discussed in campaigns. These are the nitty-gritty regulatory issues that determine how state money is spent on parks, highways, people, water and the environment and so on. The California Assembly might consider 2,000 to 4,000 bills in a session. Most touch only a few people, although for them, the impact can be huge.

Politicians know that most voters aren't focused on issues. I read in the *Washington Post* about two voters who had made up their minds. One told a candidate, "I knew I was going to vote for you because of the handshake."

He couldn't name a single issue she favored, but he admired her confidence. "You can tell something about a person from a handshake."

Another voter said, "I was impressed that she thinks she can make a difference in education. I haven't voted in a while. But I haven't had anyone knock on my door." This voter did not ask what kind of difference the candidate would make on any issues.

3. In fact, issues very seldom determine elections. Most people who get elected win because of name recognition and personality. They are well known and liked. Remember Gov. Arnold Schwarzenegger? The fact he wasn't such a bad governor was a fortuitous accident. Voters often project their feelings and values onto candidates they like without knowing what the candidate believes, just as they think they know movie stars from the characters they play.

4. We don't always get the best and brightest people to run for office. For one thing, you'd have to be nuts to want to subject yourself to the abuse you will receive. For another the pay doesn't look like much to talented people. California beats out the other 49 states on that score with the highest pay and benefits of any. As of 2013, members of the California legislature are paid $95,291 per year and $141.86 per day in session. California does not provide pensions for legislators who took office after 1990.

Understanding and accepting the above explains why you need to *keep on voting after the election.* This understanding is key to the power exercised by professional lobbyists and special interest groups. They know that it is not who gets elected that decides most issues. They know that most elections are decided on personalities, name recognition and gerrymandered districts, not issues. Professional lobbyists know that most elected officials come into office, and many remain in office, ignorant of most issues. This is not to criticize them but to recognize reality. They cannot know much about issues because there are too many.

Smart lobbyists and special interest groups also know, therefore, that it is what they do before, after and apart from the election that will determine their success at getting what they want from the political system. Political professionals and smart organizations frequently support both sides in an election to build a relationship with whoever wins. They understand that the point of supporting candidates is less to get someone to win, though that's great when it happens, and more to have a relationship with whoever wins.

Congressman Bill Posey served in the Florida House for eight years and then the senate before going to Washington. He likes to tell the story about when he was first elected and asked an experienced elected official what politics is all about. The old pro said, "Politics is just a matter of who gets what, when."

"I was discouraged," Posey said. "I didn't want to believe that." But now, after many years in office, he says it is true.

I learned reality in a different way. In 1992, I ran for the state house of representatives in a district in Charlotte, North Carolina. I was full of idealism and eager to make the system work better. An old pro I consulted told me. "Don't spend a lot of time studying the issues," he said. "Nobody will ask you about them, and that's not going to win the election anyway."

It was discouraging but true. I have talked about this with many people in office. They almost all agree that issues seldom win or lose elections. More than likely, your issues will never come up in a campaign and will not rise to a priority level for any elected official, *unless* you and your fellow stakeholders make it happen after the election. (Campaign time is a great time to communicate your issues to those running for office, however, in case they win.)

In my own campaign, after advertising, going door to door and being interviewed by the media, I received only 11 phone calls from my 24,000 potential voters. Ten were from an organized anti-abortion lobby. One was from a concerned citizen who wanted to hear my stand on issues.

My experience was typical and the result is good news: Most elected officials enter office as an empty vessel. They are ignorant. While they have campaigned on some issues, including being against taxes, "for jobs" and "for education," they probably don't know about your issues and they probably don't care. If anything, this is the root of our salvation and the reason I retain a deep and abiding faith in our democracy.

Politicians do care about one thing: getting elected and staying elected. That is and should be their primary goal. Many people will say with disdain, "She only wants to get elected." Of course she does. "He will say anything to get elected." Of course he will. Politicians' behavior is shaped by an overwhelming desire to get elected and stay elected. That gives you power.

Although they may not know or care about your issues, you can get them to care about you. Especially when you live or work in their district and are therefore a constituent. If you work in one district and live in another, you have a "twofer"—two sets of politicians who can care about you.

The most powerful moment in politics is when a voter talks with the person for whom they can vote. It's true during the campaign and it's the same after they win, especially for those with short terms. Members of the U.S. House and California Assembly run for office every two years. California state senators are slightly better off, running every four years.

That means they are always looking over their shoulder for someone who might run against them and looking ahead for voters in the next election. It is hard to understand how powerful this feeling is if you have not run for office. But I can tell you that someone who is campaigning will give his or her full attention to a voter. The person you can vote for will give you undivided attention if you are reasonable and have something to say.

This gives you an advantage over professional lobbyists and special interest groups. Politicians want your vote and, just as important, the approval it represents in a very personal, visceral way. I have asked hundreds of state and federal elected officials across the country and they all confirm this effect. When running for or serving in office, you lust not only for contact but also for approval.

Ralph Wright, who served as Speaker of the House in Vermont, put it this way:

"To a politician, when you put your name on the ballot—that's a love affair. If you lose, they don't love you.

"When you lose an election, they have said publicly, we reject you. It's a big rejection. This ain't some girl on the phone Friday night and she says, 'I'm busy,' and only she knows. This is the public saying they don't love you and it's reported in the next day's newspaper for everyone to see. By the same token, it's euphoric when 51 percent say, 'We want you to represent us.' Then you are loved."

Politicians' eyes are always on the next election, and any voter who gets irritated could start a ripple across the district. (U.S. senators are a possible exception, since they only run every six years. But even they must keep a wary eye, especially in the two years before an election.)

You may be wondering how I can say all this and also say that casting your vote is the least important weapon in your political arsenal. Your vote is very predictable just as is mine and everybody else's. You've heard of the red states and the blue states, red districts and blue districts. They are predictably Republican or Democratic. Most U.S. House districts and state house and senate districts are predictable because they have been designed to reelect the incumbent, or someone just like them. Even though California instituted a method aimed at drawing districts without regard to party, the people in the districts, and thus their voting habits, didn't change much. Presidential and gubernatorial elections are decided by the five percent or so of swing voters, those who vote for a Democrat sometimes, a Republican sometimes, or even an independent. But politicians don't know who is in that five percent, so they have to fish and fight for every vote.

So it is the lust of elected officials for election and for approval by voters—all voters—that is your most important weapon. They don't know how you voted. They don't know how anyone is going to vote. All they know is that they have to try to convert every person they meet into a supporter. It would be difficult to overstate the urgent drive in a politician to win love and admiration from every registered voter.

This gives you the solution to a major problem faced by you and everyone else: candidates and elected officials may never know or care about your issues. Your best option is to make them care about you and what you can do to elect them. Then they may care about your issues. In the following pages, I'll show you how smart individuals and organizations do it, emphasizing three major areas: (1) attitude, (2) relationship and (3) message. As for those charts you may have seen titled "How a Bill Moves through the Legislature," it's useful to know, but don't waste much time trying to learn the process. I'll tell you how to get around that.

More important is the principle that you are going to build the right long-term relationship with the people who represent you. Then use that relationship under the direction of people in an organized group, such as an association, who really know "how a bill moves through the legislature." Follow their directions and you will be all right.

CHAPTER FIVE

Your Attitude About Politics

In politics, as in the rest of your life, attitude can sink or save you. So, get your mind in the right place. In my training seminars with people who want to get something done in the legislature, I like to play a word association game. I ask the audience to give me the first word that pops into their mind when I say "politician." When a group responds with "sleaze," "crooked," "selfish," "greed," and other negative words, I know those people have very little political experience.

Other groups, often those who are most successful at getting what they want from the government, respond with words like "caring," "sincere," "dedicated," "hardworking," and "honest." Two things become obvious immediately: (1) people with little experience in politics have a negative image of politicians and (2) most people who participate in the system have a positive image.

How is it that the people who are in direct contact feel good, and the ones out of touch feel bad? How can they feel so bad about something they have no direct experience with?

After hearing this enough, I started asking focus groups questions such as, "Since you really haven't been involved, what causes you to form this opinion about politics?" The answer always came back loud and clear: the media. People who feel negative about politics have accepted what they read in the newspapers and see on television or the Internet.

In case you have negative feelings about politics and politicians, consider the things you know about—your job, your elected officials, your community. Does the media do a good job of reporting on these things? Do they give frequent, thorough, complete, and accurate reports? If you only read the newspapers and watched TV, would you have an accurate impression about your work or community?

The answer usually is "Absolutely not." That's because the media report on the exceptional, the unusual, the entertaining, the failures. The media folks—I used to be a newspaper editor—look for controversy, conflict and contention.

It doesn't meet their definition of news to report that a member of Congress or the Assembly works hard, serves the district well, listens to the constituents and tries to make rational sense out of a lot of complex problems. It's not news that your senator is honest. The news you get about politics is like much of the news you get about everything else—all you get is the exceptional, which often means the disasters. What you have hammered into your consciousness are the failures of our political system.

There's another more important effect that contributes to the negativity people express about politics. Much of what is reported is about campaigns. Campaigns are by nature contentious, adversarial and controversial. The story plays out as drama focused on conflict. This is called the horse race story: who's up, who's down, who's ahead, who scored, who didn't. If you are campaigning, the name of the game is to slam your opponent.

It's like football. It's a contact sport. It's rough and people get hurt. But it's important to recognize that it is campaigning—and the media coverage of it—that largely creates the negative perception about all politics. Keep in mind that campaigns have little or nothing to do with most issues. They have little to do with what government does.

Don't get me wrong—campaigns are important, as is voting. But campaigns and voting only decide which men and women will serve in office. Very few issues are decided in elections, unless you hold a referendum. What we are talking about—lobbying by grassroots volunteers—is what happens between the campaigns and elections. Grassroots lobbying for legislation has almost nothing to do with the things you see on TV or read in the newspapers. It has everything to do with getting what you want.

Unlike campaigns, legislative lobbying is a civilized, orderly, sane and mostly low-key business-like process. That's why you almost never read about it or see it on TV. It is dull, but it gets things done. When you get engaged, it will feel much more like your day-to-day work in which you deal with rational people in a rational way.

In some ways, politics is like the workplace. When you vote on Election Day, that's the day you decide who gets hired. Next, your unlearned, unskilled new employees, your senators or assembly members, report to work. Their success is determined by what happens in the ensuing weeks and months after being hired. You need to give your newly elected officials constant direction and coaching just like any employee. Getting elected does not mean the voters, or anybody else for that matter, has told them what to do despite the winners crowing "the voters have spoken" or "the voters have given me a mandate."

Even if they do have any kind of "mandate" it will only be one issue, and that's probably not your issue. You still have to tell them what you want. If you don't, you leave them free to do whatever they choose. They will undoubtedly be hearing from people on the other side of your issues, and if your elected official doesn't hear from you, you give them permission to go the other way.

CHAPTER SIX

Your Attitude About Advocacy

In my research into why people don't contact elected officials, one comment comes up frequently: "Elected officials are too busy doing important work to talk with me." It's true they are busy. But nothing is more important to an elected official than a constituent. Just think, who put her in office? Who is going to determine if she stays in office? You and others like you who vote in the district.

I did a grassroots training session in New York State some years back. Afterwards, I went with one of the trainees over to the Capitol to meet with her senator. When we got there, we met with a staffer who said the senator would be back shortly; he was in a meeting.

The senator was Ronald Stafford, chairman of the Senate Finance Committee. He was holding an important budget hearing, yet he left the meeting to come talk with this one woman from the district. When it was over, I asked him why he left an important meeting to meet with just one voter. Here is what he said: "Because I know that anytime I don't meet with her or any of my constituents, they are going to go back home and get on the phone and call everyone they know and tell them that I'm getting too big for my britches and I have no time for someone back home. And the next election, they may send me back home."

Elected officials who stay in office keep in mind who sent them to the capital and who can send them home. Doing this, Stafford served in the New York Senate 37 years.

Many people think politicians don't want to hear what they have to say because the politicians have already made up their minds. On some issues, it's true; you can't change their minds. Elected officials, just like you and I, have some attitudes they will not change. I call these quasi-religious beliefs. They are deeply seated matters of faith and belief, and almost no amount of logic or persuasion will change a person's belief system. Abortion, gun control, the death penalty—you are unlikely to change anyone's mind on those sorts of issues. Many times, not even the threat of losing an election can change a politician's mind about these issues; they would rather lose than change.

But the issues you will be lobbying are likely to be less visible, more specific and less emotional. They are less a matter of faith than of practicality. How shall we fund parks? Should optometrists do laser surgery? Your elected official probably knows little or nothing about your issue. They have no emotional or political stake to defend and are willing to be persuaded.

Somebody is going to help them decide. It can be you, particularly if you live or work in their district. But first, you have to persuade them to care at all. If you can convince them that enough voters in their district or enough important people in the district care, they will care. Then you have a chance to persuade them to support your position. That's a main source of power for you. (I'll explain how you can become important to your elected official when we get to relationship building.)

Even people who belong to special interest groups often fail to realize their own power. They think they don't need to work for themselves because they have a paid professional lobbyist to do the work. You need that professional, the one I call the "inside lobbyist." The professional has the power of knowledge, persuasion, personal relationship, good information, and maybe fundraising—that's significant. But the lobbyist can only vote in one district. To a politician, the importance of the professional lobbyist pales in comparison to someone who lives and votes or works in the district.

Imagine that I am your senator. I may like your professional lobbyist and respect her. But the lobbyists needs me more than I need her. I can accept her information, reject it, or just ignore it. If I kiss off or ignore your lobbyist, so what? That lobbyist can hardly try to get even with me for fear that I will remember it the next time she needs me.

But as your senator, when someone who can vote for me says people in my district care about an issue, I have to listen. I can't afford to have people back home saying negative things about me. You are a substantial member of my community and not only do I want you saying positive things about me, I really, really don't want you saying negative things. What's more, you can help me understand why something is important in my district. After all, I want to represent that district and win the next election.

Perhaps you don't advocate for your issues because you are worried about getting into controversy and somehow someone will get angry and retaliate. You are concerned that something bad will happen as a result because you've seen bare knuckled politics on TV. It's not likely.

Think about your issue. Could be education. parks, scope of medical practice, mental health, taxes, insurance or water. These issues are not like abortion or gun control, where everybody has an opinion and strong feelings and some opinions and feelings are extreme. Most issues are not the kind of thing anyone will get emotional about. No one except you and your opponents care. Most issues never even make the back section of the newspaper, much less the television.

Even the most nonpartisan, apolitical group is expected to advocate or educate to win support for its goals. Politicians want and need your expertise and experience. There is a key difference between supporting issues and supporting candidates. As long as you stick to your issues and skip personalities and endorsing candidates, you will stay out of trouble.

Despite media reports to the contrary, Americans are usually able to disagree agreeably. The media folks have to emphasize conflict and maximize the appearance of conflict or they lose their audience. Do not accept the media portrayal of politics as reality.

Another obstacle to advocacy is time. We're all so busy surviving, dealing with family and jobs; we think we don't have time to get involved in politics. You may envision "getting involved" as having to stay on the phone, go to a lot of meetings, write a lot of letters, and travel to the capital. Not so.

If you are focused on one issue, you probably won't need to write or call more than six times as the legislation moves through the process. If you make contact six times, taking less than a half hour each time, you can have significant impact. How long does it take to scribble a note and fax it or to make a phone call urging your elected official to vote yes? Is your issue worth three hours of effort?

Organizing Your Organization

Most effective special interest groups use a "key contact" system. A key contact is a person who volunteers to build a relationship with a specific politician and carry the message from the organization to that politician.

As a key contact for your organization, it would be a busy year if you were asked to contact your elected official more than ten times. That means, unless things are really hopping, you might be asked to make ten phone calls or write ten letters. That's it. Figuring a maximum of one-half hour each, you have invested five hours.

Most key contacts write fewer than four letters and make fewer than four calls or personal contacts in a year. Even if you double or triple it, you aren't risking overload. Aren't you willing to commit five to fifteen hours in the next twelve months to achieve your political goals?

If everyone who has a stake in your issue would commit those few hours, you would be unstoppable. You would have an unbeatable political machine. That's without even leaving your home or office. As for going to the capital, it can be useful and fun, but it's not necessary.

In fact, when you become a volunteer advocate for your association, your best work is done at home in the district. You can drink coffee with your elected official, attend meetings you were going to anyway such as chamber or civic club events, invite the politician to see the place where your issue plays out. It could be a park that needs funding, a hospital emergency room or anyplace you can show how people are affected by your issue. These contacts are powerful when they are arranged by constituents in the home district. Throughout this book you can see how elected officials are moved by this kind of experience. You don't need to invest time or travel. Lots of good work can happen at times and places that you are doing other things.

As we researched the reasons average citizens don't get involved in lobbying, one fear came up time and time again that surprised me. "The buildings." I chuckled the first time I heard this. But then as my focus group work proceeded, it became obvious—the buildings are a factor in alienating people. As I said, you don't have to go to the capitol or other government buildings, but there are times when it's useful. You will find it's fun. (Political fluency note: Capital, with an "a" is the city, Sacramento; capitol, with an "o" is the building with a dome on top.)

To get over that intimidation factor I started asking the question, "What is it about the buildings?" Finally it came to me: Our capitol buildings were designed to intimidate. The United States Capitol and yours in Sacramento are modeled after Greek and Roman architecture in the neoclassical style. Those Greeks and Romans weren't building customer friendly malls to attract lots of people. They were building temples to the gods. They were designed to inspire awe and intimidate ordinary people.

Picture the challenge. You walk through meticulously groomed park-like grounds, up a long flight of stairs, through tall stone columns and huge doors into elaborately decorated high-ceilinged rooms. That's if you make it through security without getting busted.

(As an aside to give comfort to those of us who live in California, if you live in New Jersey, this does not apply. The capitol looks like a seedy store. It's intimidating, but mostly because it looks like a haven for muggers. In New Mexico, they call it the roundhouse. It is. But I digress.)

One woman told me she walked into the capitol in Albany, New York, and had to fight off the impulse to kneel and genuflect—she felt as though she had walked into a cathedral. It's easy to be overwhelmed by the architecture, as well as the hustle and bustle and confusion.

So, if it's any help, most of us who don't work there every day are somewhat intimidated by the buildings. The answer is to walk in like a customer who is welcome. As long as you use common courtesy and etiquette, you will find a lot of friendly people who will help you. It won't take long to overcome your fear.

Talking to Politicians

Many people say to me, "I'm afraid to talk to a politician. I don't know what to say."

Yes, you do. You are an expert on your issue. If you are fighting for libraries, you have probably been in more of them, more times than the elected official you are trying to influence. You have seen what goes on when children's eyes light up because of a storyteller. You are the frontline trouper using your library every day. You see and live with the results of legislation that affects libraries. The same is true if you are fighting for more bike trails, more scope of practice for optometrists or different regulations for private retirement plans.

You know more than your senator or representative about how you and others are affected. That's the key to your power and all you need to talk about—your experience and expertise. Think about your elected officials. Many are lawyers. Some were journalists. Some have been Realtors. Some were homemakers. Whatever they were, they probably don't understand your issue and how it impacts people unless you tell them.

This is particularly true for those elected officials who go to Washington and live in an increasingly isolated Never Never Land. They know it. When you ask them, they always say the one thing they miss most is the day-to-day contact with real people who can express the real needs of their community. Federal house and senate members from California in particular get more and more isolated because travel back and forth takes so much time. They and their families can't help but become creatures of the place they live and work. Washington DC is not like where you live in California. You can fill their void with your stories. The same thing happens as elected officials spend more and more time in Sacramento. The result is that your elected official wants to hear from you and you have valuable information to give them.

CHAPTER SEVEN

Your Attitude About Your Rights

We seem to be a nation of complainers. We take it for granted that we have the right to blame the government for everything and to try to get the government to fix everything. But step back a moment. Where do you get the right to lobby? Most people eventually answer, "It's in the Constitution."

Of course. After thinking for a while, you might have said it is in the Bill of Rights, perhaps freedom of speech. Although you are close, it's more specific than that. Remember the First Amendment to the Constitution:

Congress shall make no law respecting an establishment of religion, or prohibiting the free exercise thereof; or abridging the freedom of speech, or of the press; or the right of the people peaceably to assemble and to petition the government for a redress of grievances.

Your right to lobby is spelled out: "to petition the government for a redress of grievances." That means a lot more than adding your name to a list at a table in a mall or online.

You remember from history class how the Bill of Rights—the First Ten Amendments—came to be written. Our ancestors had just come through a long and bloody war (about eight years) and had created the Articles of Confederation to bring the states together. That didn't work, so they came back and wrote the Constitution. But some states wouldn't sign until they added the Bill of Rights, including the First Amendment.

It's obvious, given what they had been through and what Europe had been through, that religion, press, assembly and speech would merit protection. So why did they put your right to lobby in with freedom of religion, speech, press and assembly? Because they had not had that right. Historically, the king in England ruled by divine right and could not be questioned. The citizens did not have the right to petition for a redress of grievances. The Founders understood that only if the people had the right to complain—constantly—would government have to listen and respond.

This right is one of the founding principles of democracy that separates us from a lot of the rest of the world. This is one reason people from around the world want to come here. It is one reason why I urge you to make lobbying a part of your personal and professional plans and goals. I go even further. You not only have the right to lobby, it is your obligation, your responsibility. It's important for you to let your government know what you want and don't want. It's a way of repaying those people who, 200+ years ago, gave us everything we have today. It's a way of making sure that those who come behind us enjoy the same privileges we do. When you work through an advocacy organization for your cause, you are making this democracy work the way the Founders envisioned.

As I said in the introduction, one of my goals in life is to get all Americans to contact the people they vote for. I am convinced if we can do that, we can solve every problem that faces us. Though I may not be able to get every single American energized enough to write a letter or make a phone call, I hope you will. I hope you will become one of those people who make democracy work. It all starts with your attitude—about politics, politicians and yourself.

CHAPTER EIGHT

Fifty Percent Plus One Equals Success

You can have a powerful influence over elected officials—particularly when you are talking to the ones you can vote for. But no politician would or should act just because you, or any other one person, have a great idea. They won't take up your cause since—if they are experienced—they know they only have a certain amount of political capital to spend. They won't waste it on causes they can't win.

Remember the "magic numbers" to get what you want? John McGoughlin, a state representative in North Carolina, explained it to me this way: "There are lots of good ideas out there. Really good ideas. They are practical. They will work. They will accomplish some useful social goal. But they don't have the political support to go anywhere. At every step in the process you must have fifty percent plus one or you die."

That's a nice dose of realism. It doesn't matter how righteous your cause is. If you can't show widespread support, your issue will die. Politics is the art of finding the middle, building consensus, creating a majority. One person's idea, no matter how good it is, will not be given serious consideration just because it's a good idea.

Only those ideas that have, or reasonably might have, or someone can cause to have, widespread support are worthy of becoming public policy. Setting majority rule and democracy aside, ideas without widespread support just will not work.

The way you demonstrate widespread support is through an organization or working with many organizations.

Take another look at the First Amendment: "the right of the people peaceably to assemble." One of the first things tyrants do is ban meetings. They don't want people banding together to multiply their strength. That's why in addition to petition, you got the right to create or join a group. So when you join a business, professional or environmental association, you are once again following the path laid out by the Founders of our democracy.

In fact, most often political goals are achieved through an association of people, either formal or informal (as in a coalition). If you don't represent something larger than yourself and your good idea, you are unlikely to be taken seriously.

It's like a newspaper op-ed page (that's the page across from or opposite the editorials with columns and articles of opinion). I could submit an article outlining a brilliant public health initiative to combat teenage pregnancy. I might get it published as a brief letter to the editor. It wouldn't merit anything more because what I think on that topic, no matter how good the idea, isn't worth much.

If the surgeon general or the chair of a senate committee wrote the identical article, it could get major play around the country. It would be taken seriously because it would represent some significant constituency, something larger than one person's good idea.

For purposes of this book, I assume that you are a member of an association with a public policy agenda. It could be a Chamber of Commerce, the Sierra Club or something else. No matter what your issue, if it has any chance of getting legislative attention there is almost certainly some group already working on it. Your best bet is to join that organization. This usually provides you with the next essential ingredient: the professional advisor.

Having a Coach Is Key

You must have an insider who understands the players and the process and who can lead you through the minefield of legislative deliberation. Think of it in terms of a sports metaphor: The association members are the team. They carry the ball and they score. The professional advisor, usually a lobbyist, is your coach, providing the experience and judgment to bring your talent and energy to bear in the right place at the right time.

Although a professional lobbyist is the most common advisor, I have seen instances where volunteer advocates had the time and knowledge to do the job well. Another possibility is your own elected official. If you can get her interested in your issue, she may be able to help you chart a course through the legislature or Congress, or at least point you in the right direction. But don't expect them to take up your cause and lead the charge. They have too much on their plate.

The keys to success for most associations are (1) get a professional lobbyist and (2) obey them. Unless you are focused on politics and your issue 24/7/365, you will make costly mistakes. This includes understanding the system, knowing the major players and personalities, understanding their motivations and having the commitment and time to focus virtually all your energy on the political system. It will take you too long to learn all of that, and you may never figure out how to make something happen.

The first time I tried to get some legislation passed was back in the early 1970s, when open meetings and records were a much bigger issue than they are today. Working with Common Cause, a group of us in Atlanta were trying to get the legislature to open the budget process. Our state representative, Sidney Marcus, had agreed to help us. At one point, he told us to pull back because the Speaker of the House didn't want this legislation introduced. Sidney said he wouldn't introduce it. Since we knew the cause was just and right, we decided to pressure Sidney. We started calling him. We decided if we could make his phone ring often enough, we could change his mind. After one or two phone calls, he took his phone off the hook. He didn't want to deal with a bunch of fools—particularly when so many of us were not even from his district.

Frustrated, we found a freshman representative who agreed to introduce our bill. After he introduced it, in defiance of the Speaker of the House, the freshman got squashed and stripped of influence. Sidney, on the other hand, became chairman of a powerful committee.

Later he gave us a lot of help and advice. Because of his position, he was able to help get a lot of our ideas passed into law. Unlike us amateurs, he had enough sense and experience to know what to do and when to do it in order to get something done. Because we did not factor in Sidney's experience and judgment, we were left holding our ideals and initially had gotten nothing—even though we knew we had gone after the right thing. Be smart. Get a professional advisor and follow their directions.

Two Important Players

I draw a distinction between what I call the "inside" (professional) lobbyist and the "outside" (volunteer) lobbyist. You need both. The inside lobbyist is your professional legislative representative. This person knows the ins and outs of the California Senate and Assembly or U.S. Congress. He knows the committee system. He knows the players. He knows the arcane parliamentary rules. He knows the secret handshake and the password to get behind closed doors. He could draw a chart showing how a bill moves through the legislature from memory. It's vital to have a person like this on your side.

But you, the volunteer advocate, the outside lobbyist, don't need any of that. Your skills and value lie in your ability to communicate to the person you vote for and relate your personal experience and your knowledge of how things work regarding your issue and life back in the district at home.

In contrast, professionals provide technical details. They write and edit legislation. They discuss the broad scope and sweep of politics across California and the nation. They use logic, statistics and politics to persuade. They make the case in general. They develop strategy for legislative steps as your issue moves through the process and action to achieve those steps.

Elected officials want to know three things from you: (1) How an issue affects their voters, (2) how much their voters care, and (3) who cares. No matter how worthy your cause, your elected official wants to know how many people care, how much they care and how many live in their district.

This is information that you can provide better and with more credibility than the professional lobbyist. You work and live with the people in the district—the professional lobbyist doesn't. You have a critical role in communicating your perspective about your issue as an expert who lives and/or works in the district.

All professional lobbyists with whom I have talked (hundreds of them) acknowledge this effect. They will tell you that they can be much more powerful if they have a constituent or two with them. Much of their power derives from whatever perception the elected official has of the lobbyist's constituency.

What to Do and When

Elections and legislative sessions are like tides: the ocean rolls in and out on a predictable schedule and determines where you put your umbrella and cooler on the beach. In the same way, every organization needs to develop strategies for four time frames that fit within predictable election and legislative cycles. At any given moment you are somewhere in this cycle:

1. From now until Election Day. What are you going to do in the weeks and months leading up to elections? Depending on your organization's culture, it may range from nothing to recruiting and running candidates. Just make sure you have considered the election cycle and have a strategy for building relationships and delivering your message to candidates. This could be a period as long as a year.

2. From Election Day until the start of the legislative session or Congress. This is when some of your best work can be done. Establish relationships with the newly elected. Strengthen relationships with those reelected. Lay groundwork for your legislative program. Identify key decision makers and legislative gatekeepers. Test your volunteers to see who will perform.

3. From start of session to end. What will you do in the district? Will you bring people to the capital? What sort of communications system will you use? What's your media strategy? What is the role of your volunteer advocates? Do you have key contacts in targeted districts trained and ready to respond to action alerts? Do you have a year-round organization?

4. The long haul. It may take years to get what you want, meaning that the immediate success or failure you achieve is not final. You, and all with you, must be prepared to stick with your issues through defeat and after victory. You must demonstrate a commitment strong enough to convince those in power that you are never going away.

CHAPTER NINE

Building Relationships

I assume that you're working with others in an organization and you want to have an impact on public policy in California. You will be most effective if you realize that your primary job is building relationships with those who can give you what you want. Issues come and go, and you win some and lose some. But the relationships you build will serve you for a long time, win or lose.

First, reject the negative presentations of media and assume that most elected officials run for office out of a genuine desire to serve the district they will represent. In my experience this is true, and if it isn't in a particular case, that positive approach will still serve you better. Even if a candidate runs to promote his own agenda or advocate his own issues, he soon learns that unless he is winning friends with service, he won't be in office long. So his driving impulse is to help you if he can. All things being equal, elected officials will try to help you because that's how they get re-elected and that's why they are in office.

Their problem is that they can't help everyone. Each legislator must carefully choose which issues to get behind. A member of Congress told me that voters have to understand, "We're here to represent you, not advocate for you."

The California legislature might see 4,000 bills and other measures introduced in an average two-year session. Anywhere from several hundred to several thousand pass into law. The average assembly member or senator cannot give careful consideration to more than a handful. She cannot lead the charge on more than one or two.

How can you get her to choose to represent your issue? Start by understanding her priorities and what the world looks like from her perspective. Here are the priorities for elected officials.

First, she will try to push the things she believes in, the things that were important in her campaign, such as promises made. As I said earlier, your issues are unlikely to have been part of any campaign.

Second, she will support issues important to leadership. Those who control the house and senate—as well as the governor—all have their agendas. Your elected official, the one you vote for, has to work with them to accomplish anything. It was that consummate legislator, Lyndon Johnson, who said, "If you want to get along, you have to go along." Most legislators, certainly those who are going anywhere, will back leadership because it makes the decision easy. The issues that leadership is backing don't take much time, either. One strategy is for you, your organization, and your professional advisor, to get leadership to adopt your issue. This makes for easy sailing but is difficult to make happen.

The third set of issues your legislator will push is in an area where the volunteer advocate plays a key role. These issues are the ones the elected officials' friends and supporters are interested in, issues that have the potential to be passed into law. An elected official's circle of friends and supporters become her binoculars on the world. They are the filter through which the official sends and receives information and through which she views the world. It's natural enough and we all do it. How much time do you spend listening to people you don't like, don't know or don't agree with?

No matter how hard we try, we all tend to associate with people who are supportive of us and our goals. We tend to reject or screen out our opponents. We tend to ignore people we don't know in favor of those we do. Your challenge is to get in with your legislator's friends and supporters. Then, through your organization, you can get enough other people around California who are friends and supporters of enough other elected officials to get to the critical 50 percent plus one needed to move legislation.

Relationships are critical because in the beginning, your elected official probably doesn't know or care about your issue. But if she knows you and cares about you, then she will allocate time and energy to help you. That's what relationship building is all about. If your association has mobilized enough people in this category in the right places up and down California, or in the nation, you can build up to fifty percent plus one.

This rule will help you: Never ask a politician for anything until you have helped her enough that she will welcome an opportunity to repay you. If you have done nothing for her, why would she help you, given that she has limited time and there are others with equally worthy goals who have already helped her?

So, a key question in determining your success is, how can you get your elected official to care about you? The answer will come as you consider these two questions: (1) What are her personal and political goals? (2) What have you done to help her achieve her goals? Following that line of thought, what goals of hers might you help get accomplished?

Of course, her first goal is to get reelected. Others might be (1) to pass legislation, either a particular piece or just any bill; (2) achieve recognition—she wants people to know what she has accomplished; (3) advance to a higher political office or to more power in the current office; (4) find new problems to solve; (5) raise money for re-election.

If you want to understand politics or a particular political event, keep in mind this hierarchy of a politician's needs.

1. Get elected.

2. Stay elected.

3. Get power.

4. Keep power.

5. Increase power.

Please don't be turned off by the word "power." That means the ability to do things. In the context of this book, "get power" might mean chair a committee. Then, to "keep power" you have to keep your party in majority control of the assembly or senate. That's why so much of a politician's time is devoted to raising money and helping others win their elections: so his party stays in power and he keeps his seat as committee chair. "Increase power" might mean moving into a leadership position on a better committee or some legislative office like majority leader.

All politicians have an "inside" agenda that you need to take into account. That is, within the legislative body, to get power, keep power and increase power. This explains why you see someone like Nancy Pelosi of San Francisco creating a farm bill that a great many of her constituents didn't like. She was willing to offend a lot of her constituents to defend some newly elected Democrats who needed that farm bill to get re-elected. She calculated it was worth the risk to keep Democrats in power and herself as Speaker. Now she focuses on regaining a majority in the U.S. House in hopes of becoming Speaker again.

This is important to you and your issues because your elected official has to balance their desire to help you against their desire to move up in leadership. If it's a choice between you and leadership, you may lose unless your elected official is one of the few who faces a tough re-election challenge. However, if you play your cards right, you can have a powerful friend when your elected official becomes Speaker

Support Their Goals

Each elected official will have a different set of goals. Your job, as a volunteer advocate, is to figure out what they want and help them get it.

You will stand out immediately from the many people who want something from a politician if you just ask, What are your goals and how can I help you attain them? The big No. 1 is reelection. Have you volunteered to work in a campaign? Have you contributed significant money to your PAC or to the election campaign?

If so, you will have access and receive a warm welcome. But notice, I asked, "Have you contributed significantly?" People frequently ask me how much to give. My rule of thumb is, you want to be in the top tier of contributors. You want your contribution to stand out, whether it is from a PAC or from you personally. That's one reason PACs work. They bring together amounts of money that will be remembered. When you deliver a PAC check, the politician remembers you.

As for personal contributions, they are a matter of public record, so find out what others are giving and give enough to stand out. People often tell me they don't feel good about giving campaign contributions. It feels like they are trying to buy a vote. Don't worry. That doesn't happen with legal campaign contributions. For one thing, there are limits as to how much you can give.

For the 2014 California senate and assembly races, individual limits were $4,100. Another option for your group may be a "Small Contributor Committee" which can give $8,200. (You can find all the rules at the Fair Political Practices Commission website: www.fppc.ca.gov). These contributions are on the record, on the Internet and reported in the media.

Whatever your cause or organization, finding a way to get money to candidates will help you get in the door. It will not buy a vote. It frequently happens that your opponents, the people on the other side of your issue are also giving to the same candidate, so the money from opposing sides balances out.

You're not going to buy a vote with a legal contribution, but obviously you are giving to promote your cause or interest. So what do you get for the money?

The best reason to give is that you may actually help elect someone who agrees with you. Presumably you are supporting your friends and opposing your enemies. The money you give to a campaign is used to pay for advertising, direct mail, phone bills—the things a person needs to do to get elected. One politician pointed out to me, "You're not giving the money to me, you're giving it to the campaign."

It's a good place to start: Get "good people" (those who agree with you) in office. It's also true that you cannot expect anyone to be in 100 percent agreement with you 100 percent of the time. Just because you help elect someone does not mean she will always be with you.

However, given that most issues could go either way and the state would survive, and given that most politicians don't know or care about most issues, and given that their basic impulse is to help their constituents, friends and supporters, it follows that if you are a significant contributor—either by giving time or money or raising money—you get more than access. You get a warm, helpful welcome.

I still believe that any citizen with something sensible to say can get a conversation with an elected official whether they give money or not, although it may not be easy. It is in the politician's interest to at least listen. (U.S. senators from large states like California are the exception. Hardly anyone gets to them; they just don't have the time. Getting to their staffers is the key.)

But you want more. You want a relationship with your elected official that moves from professional courtesy to friendly support. You want her wanting to say yes—and being eager to help. Money isn't the only way. For example, volunteering time to work in a campaign or work on a task force can be even more valuable. This may be hard to believe because of the way television and newspapers portray campaigns. When you see campaigns on television, you usually see the big national races or hotly contested races for the U.S. House or Senate. You see a carefully created picture of crowds of enthusiastic volunteers.

The reality, particularly at the state and local level, is different. The number of consistent volunteers, not paid staff, working in campaigns is very small. One state senator in Michigan told me she had to hire temps, not because she had no supporters but because they were all two-worker families with children and had no time.

You can become a valuable resource just by showing up. Think back to that contentious 2000 Presidential election. Remember the volunteers in Florida who completed absentee ballot applications for the Republican Party? Think about the people who demonstrated in front of the ballot count in Miami and apparently contributed to getting the count stopped. A small effort by you can make a big difference and will be remembered. You can establish a relationship and you can earn that warm, friendly access by putting out signs, making phone calls and stuffing envelopes. You can—with relatively little time investment—get on a first-name basis with your elected officials.

It helps to develop a specialty—something you like doing and can do well—that's valuable to a campaign. For example, if you are friendly with numbers and detail, learn how to keep track of campaign contributions and expenses. It's not hard or complicated; it just requires a good eye for detail and a lot of discipline. People who can do this are worth their weight in gold to the campaign and the candidate.

My specialty is signs. When I support candidates, I load up my car with signs. I pull out my special mallet—named Edna—and my heavy-duty staple gun and cruise the precincts I know best, pounding stakes and stapling signs. The mallet is named Edna after Edna Chirico, a county commissioner I supported. I met her one day while I was out riding my bicycle. I saw her putting out signs, talked to her, and asked her what I could do to help. "Put out some of these signs," she said, and I did.

Though she's no longer in office, she still remembers me. When she *was* in office, she would always return my calls.

You can be even stronger contributing volunteers as an organization. If your association helps recruit workers, you will get that friendly access after the election.

One of my favorite interviews is with an electrical contractor from Texas who lives within a couple of miles of two representatives in Congress. Every year he sponsors a barbecue, charging admission to raise funds for the politicians and inviting a huge crowd. Everyone has fun and—guess what?—the members of Congress returned his phone calls.

One group I worked with helped set up phone banks for a man running for Congress. For two weeks, they mustered between ten and twenty people every night to make calls around the district. He faced a tough fight in the primary and won by 974 votes. His name was Newt Gingrich. Four years later he was Speaker of the House and he publicly stated that no legislation harmful to this group would pass while he was Speaker. He was as loyal to his friends as they were to him.

One easy, productive thing to do is organize a site visit for your elected official. Let them come to the place related to your issue. Could be a food bank, library, factory or other business office. If you put them in front of potential voters, put them in your newsletter or get media coverage for them, they won't forget.

Once a state senator called and asked me to write a letter to the editor. The newspaper had been covering an issue and he felt he needed to show that his side had some support. It was an issue I cared about, and I was glad to do it. It took me all of thirty minutes to write it and fax it to the newspaper. They published it. Is that senator going to answer my phone call? Will he help me if he can? You bet.

Your elected official needs many things in addition to money and volunteer time. For example, simply knowing what's going on in the community is very important. Your contacts at work, at church, through your civic club and social relationships put you in touch with people and groups of all kinds. Think of the news you hear about a new company coming to town, a new issue some town council is discussing or something you read in a local newspaper. This may be information that doesn't make its way to your elected official. Some districts are huge, especially the congressional districts, and it's difficult for officials to keep up with what's going on everywhere in their district.

For example, I read in my community newspaper that a small town nearby had formed a task force on education and crowding in the elementary school. Knowing that my county commissioner probably doesn't get that little paper, I faxed her a copy of the article. I wrote a note that said, "Here's a meeting you might like to know about. If you can't make it, I can attend and take notes." She faxed me back, thanking me and saying she'd be there and hadn't known about the meeting. It took me five minutes but it was most valuable to her.

This kind of activity is especially helpful in avoiding the "out of sight, out of mind" factor. To build a really good relationship, I recommend you put it on your calendar to make positive contact at least once a quarter. Stay in front of your elected official with something that helps her so she doesn't forget. It could be as simple as a letter, a phone call, an email or a fax, but whatever it is, do something deliberately. If you see your elected official is speaking to a group, attend the meeting and shake her hand. Stand up and support her publicly.

It doesn't have to be something that advances your cause—it's better if it doesn't. Just do something to help out or show support. Granted, this may seem simple, but it works—perhaps because so few people do it. Most people, if they participate in politics at all beyond complaining, vote and that's all. When you become personally engaged with your elected officials, you stand out like a warm slice of Mom's pound cake.

An example of things few people do is a story about the mayor of the town where I used to live. He and I are in different political parties and we frequently disagreed. But he was a reasonable man and a hard worker. He'd been in office about ten years and had done well by our town in a job that is generally thankless. We were standing out in the street one day, arguing about a zoning issue. Finally, I said, "Okay, Russell, I can see we are never going to agree. But I would like to say one thing. I appreciate the fact that you have served in office and I want to thank you for serving. Even when we disagree, I know you have the town's best interest at heart."

He was shocked. He got a tear in his eye and said, "Joel, in the ten years I've been in office, no one has ever said that to me before." It didn't change his mind. But I'm always thinking about the next time—and he will remember what I said. You will stand out if you do nothing but thank your elected official for serving—because so many people never take that simple step.

CHAPTER TEN

Dynamics of the Relationship

As I said, the mayor and I are in different political parties, and this is something that comes up often with grassroots volunteer lobbyists. Can I work well with an elected official of a different party—someone whose politics I detest?

From the organization standpoint, I recommend matching grassroots volunteers with elected officials of the same party and outlook where possible. In the best of all worlds, the grassroots contact will be a mirror image of the elected official. But this is seldom possible. Don't worry. When you contact an elected official, she usually won't know what party you are in and won't ask. Even if you are in the other party and she knows it, your issue may not be one supported or opposed by the political parties.

Right now, California is what in political circles is called a "trifecta" state. That is, both houses of the legislature are controlled by Democrats and the Governor is a Democrat. Anything viewed as "Republican" faces a tough fight. If you are of a different party than the elected official you are trying to persuade, don't give up. You never know. I do not recommend lying, but neither would I suggest you walk in and announce, "I'm in a different party." If it comes up, be honest.

(Incidentally, saying you voted for her doesn't work. It sounds like you expect something in return. Oddly enough, everyone elected officials meet seems to have voted for them. I used to meet people all the time who would say they voted for me, even though they didn't live in my district.)

No matter what their party, officials know they get elected and reelected by serving people. If they can, they want to help people in their district. It's called constituent service and they know it's what keeps them in office.

As for building a good relationship, I have found it helpful to think in terms of a "favor bank." I have an account with my elected representative just as I have one at the bank, except in this one, I deposit favors. That means you have to look for favors to do. Analyze the person's goals and help her achieve them. You will maintain a good account balance by making regular deposits in the favor bank. Deposit the time you spent putting out signs. Deposit the time you stuffed envelopes. Add to your account when you contribute money.

I think of it as building up equity so I can take out a loan. Who would I like to get favors (or loans) from? In this case, I want something from elected officials. So I want to maintain a favorable balance and never overdraw my account. Before I ask for something, I want to be sure that I have built up favors that will be remembered.

If this sounds a little too contrived, a little too cynical, remember that this is the way all friendships and relationships work. We just don't sit down and analyze it. We aren't methodical about maintaining the favor balance. Like it or not, it works. Just like any relationship, there needs to be two-way giving and receiving. If that lapses, where's the relationship?

Many amateurs and newcomers think all they have to do is head off to the legislature while it's in session, make an elegant case, and go home with a victory. It never happens that easily. Politics is a long, messy process. So another important aspect of the relationship is your expectations. You will seldom get everything you want. You must be prepared and committed to the long haul. A major idea can easily take between five and eight years to work through the legislature.

Your political results will be in direct proportion to your ability to convey the perception that you and your organization are never going to go away. A basic rule is: There is only one time you lobby—year in, year out, year round. Never stop. You were here last year, you are here this year, and you will be here next year and the year after. Elected officials are less likely to invest serious time or effort if you do not demonstrate staying power.

There are also limits to what your elected officials can do even when they want to help you. In Sacramento and in Congress, anything that passes depends on a small cadre in leadership. You must get them behind you. There is little or nothing the elected officials who represent you can do by themselves. If leadership in the house or senate is against your issue, accept the fact that you have to convert leadership—no easy task.

Opposing or not going along with leadership is dangerous. If your elected representatives are going to be effective—for you and others—they must support leadership.

Yet there are times when they don't want to as a matter of personal preference, and times when they don't want to because their constituents are on the other side of an issue. Speaker of the U.S. House of Representatives Tip O'Neill recognized this effect. When he needed to pass a bill he would often have some members who, for one reason or another, needed to vote the other way. O'Neill would sit them all in the front row. If he didn't need their votes, he would let them pass. But if he did, he expected them to vote with him. He would look them in the eye and they would know the moment had come. Do you vote with the Speaker or for your constituents? Can you imagine the pressure?

One of the great strengths of grassroots lobbying is that strong support in the district can allow your elected official to vote in your favor, even when it goes against leadership. Everyone in the legislature understands you have to vote your district.

So if you ask your elected official to go against leadership or to convert leadership, you have to give a very strong reason. One powerful reason for a legislator to go against leadership, and one that leadership understands, is a strong message from the district. This gives you power because you and your organization can provide that message. Letters, emails, faxes, and other demonstrations of support for an issue from the district give politicians political cover, even to go against leadership.

Timing is also important. Legislative affairs run on a schedule. Usually, by the time the session starts, the issue train is leaving the station. You need to get on that train six to nine months before the legislature convenes. You need to give your legislator time to absorb your information, check it out, sound out other interested parties and get back to you.

When you do talk with elected officials it is unusual, in my experience, to get a commitment. I mention this because some books advise you never to leave the presence of an elected official without a commitment. All I can say is, "Good luck." No smart, experienced elected official will ever give you a commitment until the last possible minute. That's because things can always change.

In one of my seminars, a man told me he had spoken to his representative, had a good conversation, and got a firm commitment. Then the guy voted against him. When questioned about it, the representative answered, "Leadership told me to." I asked the man if this legislator was in his first term. Yes, he was—as I expected.

An inexperienced politician may make a commitment, only to find good reasons not to keep it. But even if they have to vote against you because of leadership, all is not lost: at least now that politician owes you one.

CHAPTER ELEVEN

Gauge Your Impact

As you pursue support from politicians, you may begin to see it as a sales process. Scout your prospects, qualify them, build the relationship, respond to objections and sell the benefits. In sales, you make what is called a "trial close." That is, you check out the prospect to see how you're doing. If you can't get a commitment, you may still be able to get a sense for which way the wind is blowing by asking an open-ended, nonthreatening question such as, "How do you feel about what I've said so far? What information do you need to make a decision?" The answers will tell you what to do next.

As you work toward your goal, you will see there is a hierarchy of performance you can achieve. Volunteer lobbyists tend to move through several skill levels as they develop relationships. Let me list those for you now to help you identify your level among volunteer lobbyists. It will help you understand more about your job and what you can do, depending on your interest.

Levels of Volunteer Advocate Skills

ROOKIE

✓ Make first contact with elected official.
✓ Deliver organization's message.
✓ Understand need for accuracy.
✓ Respond quickly to action alerts.
✓ Believe lobbying is honorable, effective.
✓ Become personally effective.
✓ Get to know staff.
✓ Write letter to editor, watch politician's Twitter feed.

PRO

✓ Build personal, supportive relationship.
✓ Call, contact, write, fax systematically.
✓ Become trusted information source to politicians.
✓ Report to HQ and discuss results.
✓ Participate in campaigns.
✓ Recruit others to lobby.
✓ Politician knows your name, organization, issues.
✓ Give personal money to politician.
✓ Submit Op-Ed piece or post on politician's website.

HALL OF FAMER

✓ Become trusted advisor to elected official.
✓ Politician and staff call you with requests for information.
✓ Testify at hearings; talk with media.
✓ Gather intelligence, spot trends.
✓ Raise money for PAC.
✓ Organize home-based fundraisers.
✓ Find allies for coalition.
✓ Meet with editorial board.

CHAPTER TWELVE

What Will Make Your Message Stand Out?

In Sacramento and Washington DC, politicians have no back burner. They only deal with things that are hot, burning and immediate. Back when President Bush was trying to do something about Social Security, a member of his own party had this to say in the Washington Post: "Why stir up a political hornet's nest . . . when there is no urgency?" said Rep. Rob Simmons (CT). "When does the program go belly up? 2042. I will be dead by then."

Your challenge is to craft a message that makes your issue look hot.

There are two kinds of messages to get through to your elected official. I call these the "micro message" and the "macro message." The micro message is important to the elected official, you, and the people in your district. The macro message is important to the state (or nation) and is delivered best by the professional lobbyist or leaders of your state or national organization.

Micro Message

Your part, as the volunteer advocate, is to help develop and deliver the micro message to your elected official. In most cases, it works best if the volunteer lobbyist deals only with the micro message. You are letting your elected official know your issue is important to people in the district. This way you are dealing with things you know well. This approach also means you don't have to know the technicalities of legislation or the legislative process (although that can be useful).

First we'll look at how to construct a message, then how to deliver it.

I've surveyed hundreds of state and federal officeholders asking them this question: What do you want from volunteer lobbyists? The answers come back clear and consistent: "Be accurate, be brief, and tell me something new."

Be Accurate

Accuracy means you never go beyond what you know to be absolutely, mathematically true. If you ever exaggerate, distort, misstate facts or the other side's position, you are dead. Neither the elected official nor his staff will ever listen to you again. Professional lobbyists know this rule and obey it. Volunteers sometimes don't understand it and get carried away in their enthusiasm. While they don't actually lie, they may not present the whole picture or they may exaggerate. It's easy when you care a lot—but it's fatal.

Fortunately there's an easy way out. Do not go beyond what you know to be absolutely true. Then, if you're doing a good job, you will get a great opportunity—you will be asked a question you cannot answer. And what do you say? "I don't know . . . but I will find out" or, even better, "May I have our professional lobbyist call you?"

The second answer works better because it sets up a warm call between your professional lobbyist and the elected official. You complete an important triangle consisting of the elected official, yourself (the constituent) and the professional. Generally speaking, it's better to leave complicated technical details to the professionals. That's their job; they are likely to have a better grasp of it and they will deliver a consistent message.

Your job is to deliver your part of the message—how the issue affects you, your family, your friends and other people in your community. You want your elected officials to know that you have a headache and what it will take to cure it. You want them to know that your issue—your problem—is important to their voters. If they don't believe the people who put them in office care about the issue, they are free to ignore the professional lobbyist. So knowing that people in the district have a headache is the first step to getting relief.

Indeed, your own legislator may never need or want to know the details because your solution, your bill or whatever, will be handled in a committee of which he is not a member. But he can be powerful on your behalf conveying his interest to the action committee and leadership.

Your professional lobbyist can present both the larger picture as it relates to public policy and politics and the smaller picture of technical details. Your professional is like a coach, setting game strategy and calling plays from the sideline. Only you and other grassroots activists can carry the ball and score, because only you can make it important to elected officials.

Be Brief

Sometimes, you don't get more than thirty seconds before you are handed off to an aide. Politicians are busy and always have a line of people waiting to talk with them. You may run into them at the chamber of commerce or at a party. I've seen more than one very effective communication happen as a volunteer walked from the elevator to the office with an elected official.

Be able to state in thirty seconds what you want and why you want it. If you force yourself to deliver your message in thirty seconds, you will boil it down to its essence. If you can't get their attention in thirty seconds, you probably haven't focused your message.

To develop a winning thirty-second message, ask yourself two questions:

(1) What do I want? and (2) What key reason can I cite to win support? You want your elected official to support your position. Sometimes you will have a specific bill number. Even when you do, make sure he understands the concepts or fundamental ideas that you support because specific bills can change, disappear, and merge. Start with a focused opening that hooks the politician—what you want and why you want it. Use the format: We want . . . because . . .

Imagine we are a group of principals, for example. We want the legislature to allow us to keep our soft drink machines because we use the money to fund extracurricular activities that are really important. Taking away the machines will take away $20,000 a year in activities like chorus, chess club or debate. Although it is helpful to give a complete briefing on all aspects of your issue, that isn't usually necessary. Your main goal is to wake up your elected official and let him know that this matters to important people in the district. Give him a sense of what you want and why you want it.

Then, if he is still listening, you move to the hardest part of the message.

Tell Me Something New

Unless your representative has just been elected, chances are good that he's heard it all before. Anyone who has been in office for a complete election cycle will glaze over the moment your mouth opens unless you can say something new. You will have to work hard to get him to listen.

In the case of a newly elected person, the challenge is to educate him from ground zero. Most likely, he will be eager to hear you out. In either case, the greater challenge is to cause him to remember and care. You see, the day after the election, they all come down with a disease called TIO: terminal information overload.

Politicians are swamped with issue papers, letters and personal appeals from everybody with a cause. They get on every mailing list, and at first they try to absorb as much information as possible. They quickly learn—the smart ones at least—that they have to choose very carefully and focus their efforts in order to get anything done. They can't give equal attention to everyone and they can't even give attention to all good causes. They have to pick causes that are important to them and to those who got them elected.

Your job, as a volunteer, is to cut through the clutter with something your official will remember and recognize as important. The antidote for terminal information overload is the anecdote—a story about a living, breathing (or, if it fits, dead) person affected by the issue. It needs to have as much detail as possible to make it credible: names, dates, addresses, ages, occupations—anything that will make the person and the issue real.

In the above example of the drink machines in schools, tell him how much revenue a single drink machine generates. That's easy to grasp and he probably has no idea. Then give examples of what the revenue supports: trips to regional one-act play festivals, band instruments, whatever. Whatever your issue, share a true experience from real life. The anecdotes serve an important purpose: proving the problem exists.

One of my clients told me about a group of people in Colorado who were trying to get legislation passed to prevent "takings." People in the "takings movement," as it is called, believe the government should not take property or reduce the value of property without fair compensation. This group in Colorado had introduced its legislation and even gone so far as to get a hearing. When they made their presentation, the first question they were asked was, "Can you give us an example that happened in Colorado of a taking such as you oppose?" The spokesmen looked around, paused, scratched their heads—no, they couldn't. They were laughed out of the room. The kind of thing they opposed doesn't happen in Colorado. I'm told that to this day the lobbyists at the capitol jokingly call out to the lobbyist, "Hey Bob, got your anecdote yet?"

For several years I told this story in my seminars across the country, based on the story from a client who said he was there. Not long ago, unbeknownst to me, the lobbyist in the story was in my audience. Later he came up and confirmed that it happened just as I had been told, much to his embarrassment. As for his real name, my lips are sealed.

If you can't come up with real-life situations, it may look as though you have no problem. The stories dramatize your issue, make it memorable, and give it credibility and cut through the information overload. You take statistics and turn them into real people. It's called putting a face on the story.

Politicians are people-people. While they are interested in numbers and the broad scope and sweep of things, they respond more to living, breathing people in their district who vote and who they can help. That's why the volunteer's job—your job—is to humanize the issue, to provide the illuminating anecdote that personalizes the issue, to tell the memorable story that will stimulate emotion and action. This is something professional lobbyists usually don't have because they don't live with the problem. Even if they have the story, it's not *their* story.

For example, banks have fought long and hard for the right to sell insurance. As I worked with a group of bankers to find that illuminating anecdote, most were talking vaguely about helping their customers, having a level playing field, or offering competition to the insurance companies.

All this was good, but it was abstract and the same old argument. We couldn't find a way to make it come to life. Then a woman told this story: "Our bank is in a poor neighborhood. Two times in the last year we have held the accounts for fund-raising drives to pay for funerals for teenagers who were killed. This is a minority neighborhood and funerals are really important. The families had no money to pay for a funeral. Insurance agents don't come to this neighborhood. Since we are already in the neighborhood and have relationships, it would really help these people if we could offer them burial insurance policies."

Now that is a compelling story. If I were campaigning to pass a bill to let banks sell insurance, I would put this woman and her story into a video.

I've already mentioned Ralph Wright, former Speaker of the Vermont House of Representatives. In his book *All Politics Is Personal* he tells the story of one representative he worked with: "Most of the time he drove me crazy with his 'no-tax, no-spend' votes, but I learned over time I could get him to vote for something if I could place the problem right smack in front of him. I don't mean the issue, rather, the person who would feel the impact of a vote. If I wanted his help on a foster program, for example, I would arrange for him to coincidentally run into a foster kid whom I just happened to have with me. People touched his heart, not theories. Corc [the representative] could be trusted, not if *we* believed in the deal, but only if *he* believed in it."

When you put real people into a story, you make the case for your issue. You tell them something new. The issue of giving banks the right to sell insurance has been around for many years. There isn't anything new you can say about it. But your new story can illuminate the issue in a new way. You can win sympathy and you can get your elected official to remember and care. Make your story as specific as possible. Use real names, dates, and situations. If you've done a good job, the politician may want your help getting in touch with the people involved. Do it. To make your micro message successful, (1) be accurate, (2) be brief, and (3) tell him something new.

Macro Message

This is the message you must convey to enough people in the legislature to get that critical 50 percent plus one. Usually this will be the result of a thorough deliberative process involving lots of people, lots of fact gathering, and a careful assessment of what is desirable and what is possible. Your association will develop a consensus as to what the macro message is. Sometimes I call this the "case statement." It spells out the fundamental reasons why politicians should support your cause.

While this is important, perhaps critical, it's also true that facts, logic, data and reason don't always drive political decisions. Politicians often make decisions then look for ways to justify them, such as data.

A winning macro message starts with a firm moral, practical and political foundation. Without all three parts of this foundation, it's tough to win. The stronger you can make each part, the more likely you are to get what you want. You must demonstrate clearly that your cause is moral, practical and political. Or at least make it look as moral, practical, and political as possible.

You and I both know there are lots of laws and regulations passed that would fail these tests. Conversely, many ideas people would like to pass into law seem to be good ideas, but they never get anywhere. Much depends on how you "frame" the issue—taking what you have and making it look like what everybody wants. You create the lens through which people interpret your issue. You do it deliberately, step by step, looking for these three elements.

Moral

Is it right? Is it a good thing to do? Is it in the public interest? Can you show that it is? You have to make the case. Take, for example, smoking and the regulation of cigarettes.

If you are a cigarette company, you do not argue that cigarettes are good for people. Nobody would buy that and you can't win arguing the health issue. Simply saying "it's legal" isn't much help, because the response will be, "Okay, let's make it illegal." So how can you frame the issue to win?

What do the tobacco companies argue? You've seen the ads. It's not about health; it's about individual rights. You have a right to smoke. You have the right to choose. This is called "framing the issue" and you see it all the time on television. In response to a question someone will say, "I'm glad you asked that, Dan, because that's not the issue. The real issue is . . ."

This is particularly important when you are talking about money, tax and regulatory issues that face your cause, business, profession or 501(c)(3). Politicians don't think it is their responsibility to increase your income and secure your future. You will find no sympathy unless you can frame the issue in terms of the public benefit. You don't argue that the symphony needs money; you argue that the symphony can encourage kids to stay in school and become productive citizens. Whatever you want you must show something beyond just the benefit to you, your cause or organization: Find and focus on the public benefit.

Once you frame the issue correctly, it is easier for a politician to support you. In the case of the cigarette companies, for example, an elected representative cannot argue that cigarettes are healthy. But he can argue that people have a right to choose.

You and your professional lobbyists must frame the issue in such a way that the politician can take your side and still occupy the moral high ground. The politician needs you to give him that logical framework, that position he can take when he answers questions from opponents, family and the media. You must provide the answer that allows the politician to take your side and be proud and public about it.

Practical

Will it work? If you want to eliminate a regulation or create one, and if you have shown your senator that it is the right thing to do, you still have to demonstrate that it will do the job and be cost-effective. For example, many of my nursing home clients battle with the government every budget cycle to get more money for the Medicaid program. The challenge is to show that it is necessary to spend more money to maintain adequate care. It's tough because you come very close to saying that if you don't get more money, the quality of care in nursing homes will fall below standards—which no one wants to say.

One strategy we used was to show—using the government's own numbers—that about half the nursing homes were operating at a loss. We argued that there was no way they could keep the doors open while operating at a loss and, unless the state wanted to set up its own taxpayer supported nursing home system, something had to give. It worked for several reasons. We had credible numbers because the nursing home cost reports are all audited. We could also argue that the alternative would be to set up government nursing homes, which most people understand will be less efficient than those run by private enterprise.

Practicality is important for any issue. If you want to reduce the paperwork involved in making loans, you have to show that the consumer will still be fully informed about interest rates and the real cost of the loan. Got a problem with education? What is it? How big of a problem? How many kids and teachers impacted? How much impact? Want fewer kids per class? Show how that makes a difference. When you show your idea will work, then the politician can justify his support. It's not your elected official's job to come up with the rationale for what you want. You must help with that part.

Political

Does your legislative goal have—or potentially have—widespread support? Does it serve the public interest or a narrow special interest? In other words, who cares and how much? Politicians are looking for what's in the public interest. Even if they want to help you, they must be able to make the case that what you want provides the greatest good for the greatest number. They often measure that by how many people they are hearing from and who those people are.

Did your people send emails or make calls? Did they write once or many times? How much you care will be measured in part by the effort you make delivering your message. Were you willing to travel to the capital? The effort you invest makes a statement about your concern and commitment.

Your politician will ask, "How does this help the average person in my district or this state or the nation? If it doesn't help the average person, whom does it help? How much does it help? Who is opposed? Who will be hurt?" (Remember, who cares and how much?)

As a matter of practical reality, elected officials are only going to put their energy and reputation behind issues that have some chance of winning. They are not in the habit of supporting losing causes, no matter how correct. You must show how they can get the 50 percent plus one that they will need every step of the way and how they are going to get it.

CHAPTER THIRTEEN

Delivering the Message—What Works and What Doesn't

In our surveys of elected officials, we have asked what are the most effective methods to communicate with them. Generally they say they would like to have more good communications from constituents, and they have strong feelings about what works best. But first, let's look at some things that don't work particularly well.

Petitions

A guy came to my office the other day with a petition. He said the petition was on its way to Congress. The petition urged members of Congress to allow small business people to fully deduct the cost of health insurance. I think that makes sense and I was happy to sign. I also noticed that this guy worked for an association of small businesses and he now had my address and phone number. Sure enough, he tried to get me to join.

I have no quarrel with what he was doing, although I suspect he was as motivated by the desire to sign up members as he was to fight for the rights of small business. That's because if he had been serious about the issue, he would not have used a petition. Petitions don't influence legislators. I have asked hundreds of politicians and they all confirm: petitions are next to worthless as an influencing tactic.

Put yourself in their shoes. Suppose you have 5,000 names on a petition, 50 names per page, 100 pages. I'm your senator and you give it to me and say, "Here are 5,000 people who support the idea that small business owners ought to be able to fully deduct the cost of health insurance." I take the petition in my hand. I say thank you.

What am I supposed to do? Who are these people? Do they vote? Do they live in my district? Are they real? Did they have any clue what they were signing?

I can tell you what your elected official and his staff think: People sign a petition without reading it. They think that even if the petitioner read it and understood it, merely signing a list does not represent a serious commitment. This is especially true of mass campaigns that sign up people in shopping centers and, even worse, online. Therefore politicians pay little or no attention to a petition. A petition with 5,000 names is worth no more than one letter—often less.

If petitions don't work, why do organizations carry on petition campaigns? They do it to enlist, motivate, activate and energize the people who sign. They do it to get publicity and visibility. Petitions have significant value in recruiting activists, getting public recognition and other things, but in the battle to influence politicians directly, they are worthless.

Remember, politicians suffer from a disease called terminal information overload. They are overwhelmed with input from all kinds of people, and most of it is impersonal and not very thoughtful. It's difficult to imagine anything more impersonal and thoughtless than a petition.

Mass Mail, Email and Telemarketing

In Washington DC and Sacramento, the political pros distinguish between real communication and fake communication by using the terms "grassroots" and "astro turf." Astro turf is the derogatory term for the mass-generated, impersonal faxes, form letters, emails and phone calls stimulated by corporations, associations and their PR firms. An example of this is when some associations hire telemarketing firms to call their members, give them a quick briefing, then hook them up with a member of Congress or the legislature.

This can backfire in a big way. When the person in the district talks with a staff member, it only takes a couple of questions to find out that the caller is on the phone because of the hired agency. The caller doesn't know much about the issue. It's embarrassing to the person and to the staff member. Staff reacts negatively because they have wasted their time.

The same thing is true with computer-generated faxes, emails and letters. The staff who receive them quickly detect that the message is from a computer, not a person. They not only discount it but get angry because they have to deal with meaningless communication.

Some associations set up email communications and telephones at their conventions. They corral people and tell them who to write and what to write. The phone calls, faxes, and emails pour into legislative offices where people take a look and think, "Oh, yeah, more junk from the convention." They answer it, usually, but what effect do you think it has? It's similar to what one politician told me. He said he could always tell when a preacher has stirred his flock because on Wednesday he got a load of mail. Although he answered it politely, he didn't think there was much commitment and it didn't sway him.

If these techniques don't work, why do people use them? Several realities drive this sometimes counterproductive activity: Organizations need to show their stakeholders they are doing something and it's an easy way to get people involved. The preachers need to stir up their flock and help them feel they are doing something. It's easy. The companies providing these services do a good job of selling and professional lobbyists are all looking for an easy way to get influence. The folks involved are fooled into believing they have had significant input. (This may lead to frustration when it doesn't work.)

Social Media

Nowadays most every politician uses Facebook, Twitter and other social media. They seem to post regularly on them. They seem to receive communications and respond. I emphasize "seem" because for the most part what you see is generated by a low-level staffer, perhaps an intern. The elected official will get a report of the traffic, but that's all. Furthermore, they pay scant attention to what comes in because, again, it's meaningless and from people they don't know and don't have a reason to care about.

If you look at their communications through social media, you see a lot of projection from the politician to the public, mostly self-serving promotion. Frequently they will ask for people's thoughts. However, rarely do they get anything useful back because most of the people using social media respond with generalized emotion. Seldom does anything come in that could actually shape specific legislation.

John Kennedy famously said, "Where's the smoke, there's usually a smoke-making machine." That's the way elected officials react to social media. I don't see examples where postings on social media have caused legislators to take action. That's not to say it never happens or can't happen, but I don't see it. As with any other technique, try it. If it works, keep it up. If it doesn't, do something else.

Exceptions to the Rule

There are instances in which an overwhelming number of people participate in a mass communications campaign and the pressure is too intense to resist, even though the commitment is shallow. In one famous case, Congress wanted to take quarterly tax deductions from savings accounts. The banks got millions of customers to send in preprinted cards. It worked.

But only a few issues and a few organizations are capable of stimulating that kind of action. It's also true that anything you do has some impact. You can, with enough effort and the right techniques, stir up meaningful communication. But most massive efforts produce only shallow, hit or miss letters and phone calls—with little result. All I can say is, every member of Congress or state legislature and every staff person I have talked with—hundreds of them—say these mass techniques have little or no positive effect and often have negative effect. I believe in using techniques that we know will have a strong impact. If you can cause constituents to generate thoughtful, personal communication with the person they vote for, you will get action.

Getting Personal

So, what do elected officials and their staff want? Thoughtful, personal communications from people who can help them get reelected. Something that shows a real person in the district cares. They want to know who cares and how much. Show you care about them, you care about your issue and you care a lot.

Politicians tell me—and numerous scientific surveys show—that personal contact through letters and phone calls, for example, are the most powerful methods of contact. After face-to-face, I give the edge to postal letters, especially at the state level. As for Congress, because of the ricin poison and anthrax scares, postal mail can take forever to arrive. When it does get there, one chief of staff told me, it is often "fried," that is, brittle, because it has been treated to kill anything in it. Unless you hand-carry your mail, it's problematic. In the near future I expect that everything sent will be scanned into electronic form and forwarded to Congress, so postal mail has significant limitations. That makes email and faxes your best options.

If your email is to get through, you have to be careful and persistent. Generally, before you can send an email to a member of the House or senate, you go to their website and fill in a long form that includes your name, address, city, email address and phone number. Most have some blocking system that uses ZIP codes to screen out nonconstituents and a statement such as "I am unable to reply to any email from individuals residing outside of my congressional district." According to one study, electronic messages to the House doubled to 99 million from 2000 to 2004. In the Senate, the number of emails more than tripled to 83 million. Those numbers have multiplied exponentially since.

What works? It's surprising how many politicians use almost identical words when they answer the question, "What is the most powerful communication, the one you are most likely to respond to?"

"A letter written on ruled paper in pencil by a little old lady."

I don't suggest you do that because it might come across as phony. (On the other hand, it would stand out. For example, handwritten thank-you notes have enormous penetrating power.) But the old-lady letter symbolizes what they are looking for: a real person with a real problem who cares a lot and lives in the district. A person who sits down to write a letter is expressing a serious commitment. It takes longer to write a letter than to make a phone call or send an email. Few people send a thoughtful, personal letter, so such communications stand out when they arrive.

Especially in the Internet/Tweet/email age, a written message on paper stands out and demonstrates a strong commitment. Members of Congress and their staff will tell you a paper letter is not necessary. They are simply trying to make their own life easier. For your purpose, a paper letter is most powerful because it takes time and trouble to handle, because it's unusual compared to the number of emails.

For years, I have given the same advice: Make your letter one page, covering one issue. Just tell the politicians what you want and why you want it. However, as I continue probing to find what works best, I get more examples convincing me that a thoughtful, personal, really good, long letter will get really good, long consideration. Staff and elected officials alike have cited examples of single letters that were so compelling they had to hold a meeting to answer them. The letter raised good issues and made them think.

Once I was standing with a group of people in Austin talking to state representative Patricia Grey in her office when she noticed a name tag. She said, "You sent me a letter, didn't you. [He nodded yes.] I haven't responded yet because it was such a good letter I haven't had time to think through my response." She said the letter raised so many questions that she had been thinking and researching for two weeks in order to answer him.

That's powerful. That kind of consideration is about as good as it gets.

A long, thoughtful letter carries a heavy weight of commitment that must be answered. It also stands out because almost all others are short. But it must be a good letter, full of facts and persuasive argument, as well as meaningful detail from the politician's district or state. Of the letters I have seen, the worst are written by lawyers and lobbyists. They read like legal briefs. They lack personality and a personal touch. They are simply a position paper in letter form. This format has a place, but not coming from a grass roots constituent.

If you get an action alert from your organization, personalize it with your own words on your own letterhead, using your own examples. Many groups nowadays send out talking points and ask you to select those that have meaning to you and rewrite them. That's a good idea.

Some people take an action alert or sample form letter, write their legislator's name at the top and put their name at the bottom and send it. Don't laugh—I have seen letters that arrived in Washington with a computer code salutation (Name) (Address) (City) (State) (Zip) crossed out and the recipient's name written in. At the bottom, still shining through the ink, were the words (Your Signature), dutifully crossed out with a real signature nearby. Needless to say, that doesn't meet the standard for thoughtful, personal communication.

Some people used to use preprinted postcards that way. Sign your name and drop it in the mailbox. I'm not saying it has no effect. Enough postcards at least indicate that the issue has a constituency full of people willing to sign a postcard. It may get some attention. But it only works if you can produce tens of thousands of those—and most of us aren't usually engaged in a mass campaign that can produce those kinds of numbers.

What works is a personal, thoughtful communication from a constituent. Let's call it a letter, whether it's electronic or something else. It can be as simple as three paragraphs:

Tell your politician what you want,

Cite an example featuring a real human from the district,

Make the ask: Will you . . .?

You will probably get a form response, maybe even a robo response that looks like no human saw your letter. That's okay—particularly if it seems supportive. If you get something back that is so vague it gives you no clue, here's a powerful technique: Send another letter, only this time ask a question he cannot answer in a form letter and call to see that the letter was received. Make sure to get the name of the person you talk with and —politely —state that you need an answer. Sometimes a politician is trying not to state a position or give you an answer, sometimes the staff is just lazy or not paying attention.

Sometimes, they just don't want to say they aren't going to answer or that the answer is no, I won't support your position.

At the very least, you will make some staff person think through a response and perhaps have a discussion with a more senior person. Getting them to construct the form letter is a good first step toward winning support. The presence of a specific form letter is a sure sign they are hearing from the district. (Their form letter to you is good. Your form letter to them is bad.)

Here's another secret for a powerful letter and especially an email. Begin your letter by accurately stating the number of the district you live in. (You live in a numbered district for your California assembly member and senator and federal representative. For United States senators, your address will show your state.) When you do this, you automatically lift yourself out of the pack of passionate, but uninformed constituents.

You show you are politically savvy and a serious· player. Not one voter in 10,000 knows the number of the district they live in, even among those who know the name of their representative (and that's a very small group too). Elected officials know their district number and will respect you when you speak their language.

When you send your letter, give them permission to call you late at night or on the weekend and include your number at home and your cell phone number—particularly if your politician is in session.

Elected officials work long days; often the only times they have to call are on weekends and at night. Your willingness to allow this not only makes their lives easier, but it also shows that you are committed beyond normal working hours.

Former U.S, Rep. Wally Herger (R-CA) suggested to me that people who want to send a letter on paper could just bring it by the local district office. "We send a bag of stuff to Washington almost every day."

What is a complete waste of time for you and members of Congress is for you to go to their website, fill out their form and use a phony ZIP code that is in their district. They will mail you a letter, it will be returned and they will dismiss your email.

Faxes

I like faxes. They are fast and easy. The only downside is the quality depends on the printer where they arrive and they will be in black and white. Your letterhead, particularly if you are writing on company letterhead, may have more impact if it is in color. Sometimes your fax isn't even printed out, just saved as a computer image.

Elected officials tell me they like faxes because they are easy to work with. They often write a note on them and fax them back. One thing that seems to work well is to send something timely from a district newspaper with a note on it. Chances are good you will get there before the papers do and your note takes on added value. You are helping them and they will remember you.

When you send a fax, send it to the right person by name. This means finding out who on staff handles your issues. Then call to make sure the right person got it. Legislative offices are not always the most organized places and paperwork gets mislaid a lot. Sometimes faxes don't arrive because of technical problems and sometimes they just get lost. The person you are sending to may be gone. Your follow-up call gives two impressions and doubles the chance that the right person will see it.

Almost every computer in operation today has the ability to send a fax straight out of word processing software such as Microsoft Word.

You must be hooked up to a phone line, but you can do this easily by unplugging the line to your phone and plugging it in to your computer. Then this usually this works by hitting the print button and choosing fax as the printer. This allows you to easily create a personal letterhead if, for example, you don't want to use your office letterhead in a political letter. Because it comes straight out of your computer, it gives the best possible quality coming out of the fax.

When I send letters like this, I sign my name using a script font in 24- point script. It looks like this:

Joel Blackwell

That may not matter, but to me, it looks more personal than a typed name.

Phone

Legislators love the phone because they can have a quick two-way dialogue.

But it's often hard to reach them during office hours. If you call, get focused. Make notes about what you want to say before you call. Here's a checklist.

- ✓ Primary objective. What do I want to happen?
- ✓ Secondary objective. What will I settle for?
- ✓ What points am I going to make to get the results I want?

✓ What open-ended questions can I ask to keep the conversation going?

✓ What exact words will I use to ask for what I want? Write down your exact "ask."

✓ What is the likely response when I make the ask and how do I respond?

✓ What questions will I be asked?

One thing I observe when I watch people make phone calls is that they often get nervous and talk too fast. You don't have the advantage of using your own body language or reading theirs, so slow down. Speak distinctly.

Make sure they know who you are not only by giving your name slowly and clearly, but also by anchoring them with an image they will remember: "We talked at the chamber meeting in April" or "I sent the article on taxes two weeks ago." The politician may be standing in a restaurant or hallway. They get so many calls that if they don't know you like a family member they may not understand who you are.

If you make your pitch and she isn't asking questions, get off the line—you haven't engaged her. Follow up with a postal letter, email or fax. Reiterate what you meant to say and what you thought you heard in response.

Many times you will need to leave a message on voicemail. I love voicemail because I've got my message ready and can be pretty sure I have their attention for thirty seconds until I leave my number.

I state my name and phone number v-e-r-y slowly at the end of my message and then repeat it. It is amazing how many people compliment me on this. In contrast, I have gotten many voicemails where the caller, so used to leaving his own number, speeds up and leaves something I can barely understand. Make sure you give your name and number carefully and slowly. Repeat your name and number, especially if you are on a cell phone. You want your politician to call back. Be sure to say, "Call me anytime."

What About Email?

With the growth of email and the "slowth" (sorry, but it's true even if I had to invent the word) of postal mail and especially since the anthrax and ricin scares, more and more people are using email. What staff and politicians say is that they get it and read it, and they like the ease of response, but they discount it compared to hard copy mail. I think that's because it looks and feels transient. It lacks permanence.

The volume of email is increasing to the point where much of it passes untouched by human hand and barely scanned by human eye. One estimate from the Congressional Management Foundation indicates the House of Representatives alone is receiving more than 200 million emails a year. There is no way to consider that many messages.

The foundation reports that the bulk of such messages are generated via advocacy campaigns by the 5,000 to 10,000 associations, nonprofit organizations and corporations that have websites devoted to this purpose.

The foundation found that "a sizable number of offices are unable to respond to constituent emails with pre-existing responses in less than a week." When an office does *not* have a pre-written response, it can take three weeks or longer to reply.

Others conclude the same thing. An article in the *Washington Post* by John Schwartz was headlined, "Sometimes Email Just Doesn't Deliver."

Schwartz quoted activist Jonah Seiger, who works for a consulting firm called Mindshare Internet Campaigns: To make an impression in a legislator's office, "it is very important to make noise. Email doesn't do that."

Electronic mail, Seiger said, "has no weight. It has no mass. It comes in quietly and gets filtered by computers." American University and Bonner Associates did a study on email and found that it is substantially discounted. One flaw that staff people cite about email is that email addresses don't tell where a person lives. A majority of staffers I talk to disregard email—delete it or send a bland automatic response—unless they have some clear indication the person lives in the district.

Almost every member of Congress has a website and on that website they stress that you should not correspond unless you are a constituent. The use of email is generational and evolving. One politician told me he never responds to email. "If I do, they send me another note. I respond again. They respond again. It never ends. So I just send a letter and that's it. That's all I have time for."

But this is changing rapidly and email is clearly the wave of the future. It can work. When you are using email, it is even more important to signal in the subject line that you live in the district. Something like "Message From Joel Blackwell in Arlington." Give your name, town and address right up front of the message so they can know it is from a constituent.

However, the politicians, especially in Washington, prefer you to go through their website and use their form. Then your information goes into their database.

Some associations have the same capacity, so sending a message from your association's website works as well and allows the association to track it. However you communicate, make sure your organization gets a copy of your message and the response.

CHAPTER FOURTEEN

Preparing for Person-to-Person Communication

While I am a great believer in letters, nothing beats an eyeball-to-eyeball conversation. Politicians tell me, "It's hard to say no when you're looking them in the eye."

Before you have an oral communication—in person or by phone—I recommend you take out a 4 x 6 card. Write down specifically what you want to happen, for example: "I want you to vote for House Bill x." Give three good reasons why your elected representative should support it, three ways it will make a difference in the district. Write down an example of how it's working, or not working, or will work. This example should be concrete, specific, and about a specific person that you can name (the anecdote).

For example, I was working with convenience store operators who wanted to pass a state law requiring mandatory ID checks for the age of any person buying tobacco products.

There was a law in place making it illegal to sell tobacco products to anyone under eighteen. But it was often ignored. The police had just run a sting operation in which they dressed up a mature looking sixteen-year-old girl and sent her around to buy cigarettes—which she did. Then they arrested the clerks.

I suggested the store owners could make a good case that it was unrealistic to ask minimum wage clerks to be the enforcers and to have to decide who to ask. It was especially unfair to punish them for what could be an honest mistake. It would be much easier to make everyone show an ID.

When trying to convince a politician, my rule is to focus on the people affected by the issue. In this case, that meant I had to tell the story of the clerks, bring them to life not as bad, uncaring people, but as mostly young, not very well educated low-wage earners struggling to get by, often rushed, worried about their families, facing a line of people—all in a hurry— wanting to serve them, to do a good job. They don't want to get into an argument. It's easier for them to just sell the cigarettes instead of asking for ID. I had to talk about the sting and ask the question, "What good did it do anyone to lock up a clerk or fine them?"

Then we proposed an easier, better way to keep tobacco products from the kids. Make everybody show an ID. Put the burden on the buyer. If kids are faking their age, arrest them, not the clerk. You will always make your case more powerful when you show a politician a real problem affecting real people in their district and give them a solution.

Be accurate. Be brief. Tell them something new.

Checklist for Meeting With Your Elected Official

Everything on this list covers something that I have seen cause a failed meeting. Yes, it is long and detailed. But think about how much time and effort you have put into the effort to get a meeting with your elected official. Then think about the payoff if you get the desired result. Is the payoff worth the few minutes you will spend going over this list? How important is your goal?

I have seen many meetings with elected officials end in frustration and anger because the participants approached the meeting casually and without planning. This list is designed to help you succeed.

1. Get clear in your own mind about what you want to achieve. Usually you will be visiting as part of a coordinated effort through an association. You will have an issue and information about the issue to bring to their attention. You should have a specific assignment from your organization such as:

- ✓ Present information and ask for a response or ask for support of a particular bill or concept.
- ✓ Get your targeted elected official to contact another elected official and ask for action, such as a vote in committee.
- ✓ Become a cosponsor.

If you cannot say precisely what you want from this meeting, ask the question: Why are we doing this? If you cannot come up with an answer, maybe you shouldn't have a meeting.

2. Make an appointment. If the association has made your appointment, confirm it. If not, call the office where you are meeting, and ask for the appointments secretary or scheduler. She may want to know in detail what you want to talk about, so be prepared to explain. Think of it as practice pitching your story. It's good to lay your cards on the table early, since no one in politics likes surprises.

3. When you get an appointment, follow up with a confirmation letter or email and send a copy to your organization. Anytime you send an email, ask for a response or call to see if it was received and read. I often put in the first line "Please hit reply to let me know you got this."

4. Inform yourself before the meeting. Gather biographical information on your targeted elected official and staff. The more you know about the people, the better you can relate to them. Association staff may provide you with extensive, detailed information. If you haven't received it, ask for it. You can get what you need from the Internet, either from the elected official's site, newspaper archives, or a general search. It's a good idea to learn to do this on your own and to keep an eye out for information on TV and in newspapers back home. You only have one or two politicians to track and your association staff may have to monitor the entire legislature.

Get names of staffers you may encounter, their job titles and backgrounds. Get directions to the office and the office phone number in case you get lost. Make sure someone in your party has a cell phone that works.

5. Help the elected official and staff prepare for your meeting. Call and ask who is handling your issue. Send information that supports your case, as much as you wish, with an executive summary no longer than one page. (A staffer told me no one in Washington had read anything longer than one page since the typewriter was invented.) State what you want, why you want it, and what it means to the district and to you personally. In a follow-up call, ask if they need any more information and give them permission to call you any time at home or at the office. Make sure they have your cell phone number.

6. Prepare yourself. Get your organization's issue paper and review it. However, keep in mind that nobody expects you to be an expert on legislation. Your job is to be the expert on your little piece of the issue *as it affects you.* If you can give the broader picture, that helps. But your priority is to tell your elected representative how your issue plays out in the district and in your life. You are an expert on what's going on in your own life and industry or profession, and that's what they need to hear from you. Find out if any committee consultants have ever prepared an analysis of the issue. These are available online.

7. Find out what position your targeted senator or representative has taken on your issue in the past. Has this issue or anything similar come up in committee or for any kind of vote?

8. Find out what the next step is in the legislative process (introduce the bill, committee hearing, mark-up, etc.). Your professional lobbyist will know. Your targeted elected official may not know where your issue is in the legislative treadmill and will probably ask. You also avoid the embarrassment of learning that your bill has already been passed or defeated.

9. Take an index card and write down, as specifically as possible, what you want from the elected official. Put down three or four reasons why the issue is important in the district and to you. What is happening or will happen to real people? Picture a specific person who is or will be affected. Jot down key words to remind yourself how this person will be affected. Be able to make this person come alive with a name, age, job, address and so on. The story about a real person will be what they remember most of the time.

10. Get ready for culture shock. The staff you will encounter in the legislature and Congress may be younger than you and of a different outlook and ethnic background than the people you normally deal with. Especially in Washington, you may find yourself sitting down with a twenty-something wearing baggy clothes who looks too young to be dealing with weighty matters. Avoid displaying shock or commenting on her age. (One of my clients came out of a series of meetings and said, "My God, the country is being run by children." It's true.) Regardless of her youth and inexperience, this person is in a position to help or hurt you. Show respect.

11. Take two other people. Although there may be internal reasons that force you to take more or less, taking too many people is the most common mistake people make, according to staff and elected officials. (I have had some express surprise that so many people came all this way, so maybe numbers do count sometimes.) Among other things, you will often be in a tiny, cramped space that has difficulty accommodating even three bodies, especially in Sacramento. No matter how many people you have, assign the following functions:

- ✓ **Presenter:** delivers the message and asks for help. Does most of the talking, working from 4 x 6 card or other notes. Keeps conversation on track and focuses on purpose of meeting. Has practiced and rehearsed the message. Stays on message and gets conversation back on message.
- ✓ **Secretary:** handles papers, hands over background material as needed, gives a list of volunteer advocates who are present with names, employer (if relevant), mailing address (home), and phone numbers. Business

cards are okay, but put your home phone and cell number on them. If you use business cards, gather them before the meeting and hand them over in one stack all at once (no fumbling through purses and billfolds).

✓ **Observer:** takes notes of what is said, any requests for more information, promises made. If staff or politician says she will get back, ask when and let her know you are writing it down. You have a right to expect a prompt follow-up. Good notes equal power. Don't worry that staff will feel offended. This is a business meeting. Just say, "We want to make sure we follow up on everything."

Look at body language and facial expressions of the targeted elected official and staff. Are they fidgeting, looking at watches, answering the phone? Are they merely polite or genuinely interested? Was the meeting ended with a preplanned interruption? What was the tone of the meeting?

These things may tell you more than the words spoken. Watch to see if the listener really understands what is being said. It's okay to interrupt and suggest going back over something to make sure it is clear. Notice what kind of notes the staff and/or elected official are taking. Some are compulsive and take reams of notes. It always concerns me that they may not be listening, that perhaps the note taking is for show.

I like to hold back position papers and other written information and let them know up front that we will be providing those later. I would rather have them listening and not reading or taking notes.

I was once with a lawn care group talking to a member of Congress when they delivered what for them was a central article of faith about chemicals on lawns: "The dose is the poison." To the people in the industry, this was like saying

"Do unto others . . ." They knew that lawn chemicals in proper doses are harmless but most people overuse them with the idea that more is better.

But the congressman didn't move. I interrupted and said, "Congressman, they just said something important and I wonder if they made it clear?"

"I have no idea what that means," he said.

We were able to back up and run it by him again with an explanation. At the end of the meeting he had the central points we had come there to make.

12. Take care of business. This is not a social gathering—it's a business meeting, very much like a sales call. While you don't want to be brusque, you do want to use your limited time well, which is another reason to keep the group small: Introductions take a long time and everyone may feel they have to chat. While you want to follow the lead of the person you are speaking with, remember you have a purpose and an agenda. Say hello, give a brief introduction and a list of who is there with biographical information. Then, get to work. State what you want and why you want it.

13. When you get a signal that your time is up, say, "Let me check my notes to make sure I said everything I came here to say." Then pause carefully. Look at your 4 x 6 card and think: Did I ask for what I wanted? Make sure you haven't missed anything, especially the ask. If you need to, restate your position and ask for what you want.

14. Ask the staffer something like this: "When will you speak to Representative Smith and let him know what we said?" You might give the staffer a personal note with your home phone number and say, "Will you give this to her? Since we haven't been able to meet in person, I would like to talk by phone." Remember, one of the jobs of staff is to screen out people, to protect the elected official's time. You need to be assertive in showing that you want to speak with your elected official, if not now, then soon. I have had staffers tell me that sometimes they just take information and file it away. This is not what you want.

15. Follow up. Send a note of thanks to all concerned, including the relevant staff, receptionists, and so on. Briefly reiterate what you and your observer heard in the way of results. Thank them for support or urge reconsideration as appropriate and assure them that any promised follow-up will be coming soon.

16. Call or send a report to your association headquarters. This increases the value of your meeting many times and helps your lobbyist plan strategy.

Two Important Tips

First, never threaten or use language that can be interpreted as threatening. Statements such as, "We helped you get elected last time," "We have a lot of voters in our organization," "This will get a lot of votes," will make your politician defensive and turn him off immediately.

Anyone in office already knows the political reality. Not only is it unnecessary, but it will also be regarded as crude, rude and amateurish. If you have the power to intimidate, you do not need to say so—your politician already knows it. If you don't have it, you will look foolish. By the way, you almost certainly do not have the power to intimidate an elected official. They will probably get reelected—with or without you.

Second, communicate with a purpose. Some people call or write so often and about so many topics they are considered slightly daffy and lonely. "Don't be a pen pal," said one staffer. Writing about every topic that strikes your fancy will turn you into a pen pal. Staff and elected officials think of constant communicators as pitiful, amusing and irritating.

Which brings me to a question people often ask: How often should you communicate? As often and as long as you have something useful and new to say, it's okay. But just repeating the same stuff quickly becomes an irritating nag and is counterproductive. My gut feeling is that you need to be in front of staff and politicians with something useful and/or helpful—or in person—four to six times a year just to be remembered.

Elected officials and staff in many ways are like check-out clerks at the grocery store. They are feeding people past a scanner like cans of fruit as fast and efficiently as possible. Beep. Next. Beep. Next. Beep. Next. You want to be the can of fruit that doesn't scan, that has to be considered, price checked, thought about and processed personally. The secret to that is: Become a human.

One of the most effective leave-behinds I've seen was created by Chuck Johnson of Farwell, MI. Chuck is an avid motorcyclist. He had been trying to get to see U.S. Sen. Debbie Stabenow without success. He thought it might be that she didn't have time to talk with a "biker."

Motorcyclists have an image problem with people and politicians who don't know them. So Chuck created on his computer and brought to Washington an 8 1/2 x 11 bound booklet to leave with members of Congress. It contained his resume and color photos.

The first page told about himself in considerable detail in resume format. Then he had pictures of his wife, a Methodist minister, in her clerical robes standing beside the church sign. Pictures of him on his motorcycle, with his grandchildren, and finally of himself on the motorcycle in a parade with a huge yellow man-size chicken character on the back, the sort of mascot you see at a football game. The parade in the pictures kicks off an annual chicken barbecue in Farwell.

Chuck reports that a staffer gave this handout to the senator, probably with some amazement. Senator Stabenow thumbed through and realized that she had walked in that parade and seen the chicken character and Chuck. She got in touch with him and he was finally able to speak with her.

He had made a personal connection by becoming a real person.

I don't know what's going to work for you. But I do know it is important that you become something more than just a title or a business card. You must help staff and elected officials remember you as a multidimensional person who is part of the community. You have family, activities, and other connections that make you part of the community. In explaining this, you may find some common bond with the person you are speaking with. At the very least, you become more memorable.

Whatever your cause, make sure staff and elected officials know how many stakeholders you have in their district: employees, people served, customers, members, patients— any people touched by your issue. Paint a picture of an organization and people the politician will know about and care about.

PART II

The People

The following commentaries come from people actively engaged in making things happen in the California legislature.

Whether these comments are from legislative staffer, an elected official, a lobbyist, an academic researcher or a volunteer advocate, you will see one consistent theme:
You can have significant Personal Political Power.

The Perfect Triangle

Here are three Californians that tell you much of what you need to know to get what you want from government. Their stories are important because you get the point of view of a professional lobbyist, a guy who runs a small business and a member of Congress—and they are all connected.

Politics is all about the people who make our democracy work: politicians, lobbyists, advocates and staff. Professional lobbyists are the least understood and most maligned participants. In my own experience, they are almost all highly ethical people who believe deeply in the process. Sure, there are bad apples who break the law, just as there are in journalism, law, medicine and your business or profession.

But a lobbyists' only currency is their credibility and that, plus a host of disclosure laws and regulations, keep them at least as honest as any other profession.

The same is true of elected office holders, even though we get frequent examples of immorality, bribery and dishonesty.

No matter how discouraged you may get, or disgusted, at the behavior of the few, keep this in mind: If you drop out, you leave the field to your opponents.

This triangle—lobbyist, constituent, politician—is the strongest structure in legislative lobbying. When you put all this together, you can make things happen.

Don Campbell

Don was for many years an electrical contractor. Then he shifted gears and was executive director of the Northern California chapter of National Association of Electrical Contractors at the time of this interview. In 2014 he took the same position with the Southern Nevada chapter. He is, among other things, a professional lobbyist. Here is his story in his words:

Back when I was a contractor, some of us had gone to Washington, DC to talk with Dennis Cardoza (US Representative from California). We met with a staffer across the hall from his main office in a small room, which was really a utility room. It was very uncomfortable, un-air-conditioned, and we sat at a card table on folding chairs. At the end, we thought all was lost, that we'd wasted our time; our return on investment was nil.

Then Dennis Cardoza walked into the room. He was passing by and stopped in to see who we were. He's a Democrat who wasn't quite on board with our stand on leasehold improvements. I told him a story about leasehold improvements and the problems we had.

When I finished, he pointed to the staffer and said he wanted to co-sponsor the bill we wanted. It ultimately passed

We hadn't expected to see him, so it was a chance encounter, but by the same token, we had to be there to make it happen.

If you think there is going to be change without a relationship and without some energy behind that relationship, it doesn't happen. The only way to affect change in the political process and get what's good for your company and good for all contractors is to get involved in the process.

[Now that he is an association executive] When I talk to a politician on behalf of NECA, I do so on behalf of many contractors. Even so, when a contractor—who is a constituent of a politician and an employer who employs people in the politician's district—talks to them, it means more to the politician.

A contractor has significantly more influence than a chapter executive has.

A contractor is not a hired gun going out to do something somebody else asked them to do or to say what somebody wants them to say. They talk about real life stories and real life issues that politicians are interested in.

Politicians live in a world that is isolated, so they are interested in what their constituents want and need from them. They (the politicians) want to serve. They are serving their country in a way they believe in and they want to do what is right for their constituents.

The political process is like every other process in everything we do, in religion, in business, in everything, it's all about relationships.

Relationships are built on encounters, opportunities to speak and to be heard. NECA's issues are contractor issues, and those issues are best communicated by contractors directly to the politicians in their area. You can't do it remotely from Washington DC or by hiring people to speak for you. You have to get engaged and involved yourself.

One of our contractors, Gary Walker, held a fundraiser for Ellen Tauscher, his member of Congress. It was a great event where we not only had an opportunity to sit down and get to know her, but to have three and half hours of quality time to discuss issues that were important to all those who attended. She had a lot to say, and she also listened.

Like all politicians she has staffers that manage her time and try to protect her time, to get her in and out in an appropriate amount of time. This dinner was such a great event, her staffers were pulling her out and she didn't want to leave. She was very engaged.

I don't think contractors understand how easy it is to get involved. The fundraiser Gary did wasn't that difficult. It takes some organizational skills and you have to send out invitations. However, with some effort, you get a quality event and this one went off really well.

If we could have ten contractors in each congressional district doing what Gary did, we would have more impact and influence than you can imagine.

The contractors have the stories that have the impact. It's hard for me to sit in front of a politician and tell a contractor story. Stories are what politicians relate to. They can understand them. They can repeat them and use them to convince others. It's amazing when you sit down with a politician and tell a story and then you watch C-SPAN and you hear them telling that story on the floor of the Senate or the House. It's an amazing experience and those who have gone through that process will do it over and over again.

Gary Walker

Gary owns an electrical contracting company in San Leandro, California. He was in the Navy, served in the Naval Reserve and was called up and served a year in Iraq. He's a member of the Northern California Chapter of NECA. Here is his story in his words:

I had served on my city council, so I had some political experience. We had a local political action committee and I was active on that. Then I got involved in NECA's national PAC. Later I got to know Rep. Ellen Tauscher.

That came about when I had a personal issue I needed to resolve and I went to her—actually her staff—and they resolved it very quickly. Since then, I've been highly involved in working with her and for her campaign.

I've represented our chapter of NECA in Washington on four occasions. Last year I represented the chapter on multi-employer pension plans.

I feel very comfortable talking to her. It's just like talking to my neighbor. She's very easy going and doesn't have a lot of walls around her.

We had a dinner party at my house for her and I brought in some people to speak with her. They all felt pretty much the same way. I invited local people, some from IBEW (International Brotherhood of Electrical Workers) and other NECA members.

We had 18 people show up. When I invited them I told them it was a chance to discuss issues with our local member of Congress. I wanted to get a smaller group. I didn't want it so large that people couldn't have a one-on-one conversation with her.

So we did a $500 per plate dinner. I hired a chef and had the dinner in my home. I had a goal of raising $10,000 for her. We had six people who couldn't come, but three of those sent money. This was the first local fundraiser for her in Solano County.

It wasn't a lot of trouble, but it was some. You have to get out the invitations, call people, make up a menu, make sure you have the right number of plates and glasses—things like that.

I think it went very well because her staff kept grabbing her and trying to pull her out the door after about three hours and she wanted to stay and talk to everybody.

There were a lot of issues: NECA was interested in the multi-employer pension plan and we had a local sales tax increase to pay for roads that a lot of people cared about. It was a mix of NECA/IBEW issues and other local issues.

When I call her office, I get an answer. If I call and ask to speak to her, she speaks to me. When I went to Washington, she met with me. In the past she has come to meet with our whole chapter. We didn't go to her office; she came to meet with us at the hotel.

We have a really good rapport with her.

What it comes down to is, are you part of the problem or are you part of the solution? You have to be involved with them (elected officials) locally. If you are not, they are listening to somebody else. They have so much on their plate, and I can tell you as a former public official, it's impossible for them to know everything. It's impossible for them to know all the answers, unless you tell them.

What happens is, they get put into a box because their staff is telling them something, or somebody else is leading them on about what's important. If you don't spend time with them, they are never going to know your issue.

Ellen Tauscher

Rep. Ellen Tauscher represented California's 10th Congressional district, which includes San Francisco's suburbs in Contra Costa, Alameda and Solano counties. She left that office to serve as the Under Secretary of State for Arms Control and International Security Affairs until February 2012. She served as Special Envoy for Strategic Stability and Missile Defense at the State Department and now is Vice Chair-Designate of the Atlantic

Council's Brent Scowcroft Center on International Security. Here is her story about being a member of Congress:

When you become a public official, you have to understand there are demands on your time and it's necessary to be accessible.

I can't go to the Safeway for a quart of milk without spending 20 minutes with somebody who wants to talk about something. It's part of the job.

Going into a home environment, for a fundraiser or just a meet-and-greet, reinforces the sense that you are accessible, that you know you work for them; you are there to hear what they have to say.

When the districts were redrawn in 2002, Solano County came into my district and Gary was one of the first people I met from there. He offered to help my campaign.

Recently he had a small dinner party for me at his home. Those are fun events for me because it takes me out of my normal business atmosphere. It also helps the people who come to these events because they are more at ease. It's not a formal situation. People can chitchat; they don't feel they have to talk with me all the time.

I also know that I don't have to be "on" all the time or that it's specifically a business meeting. It's much more of a congenial way for people to get together. That's why many organizations that have a grass roots operation to influence Congress, as they should, have these kinds of events—and they are very successful. People feel comfortable. The elected people feel that, in a home environment, it's more conducive to having a conversation. You get to know people better; they are more at ease.

And Gary serves the best food. Fabulous! It was a wonderful evening. Many of the people there were people I had worked with for a long time. It's nice to let your hair down. It's nice to have a glass of wine. Not everything is about politics.

I don't have to agree with my constituents all the time, but I do have to listen to them all the time. Even though sometimes I have to bite my tongue, I have to listen respectfully. If they maintain that respect for me, then maybe we can come to an agreement or decide not to agree and go on to something else.

This is about people understanding that they have access and that there needs to be respect on both sides. It's about information—not only for us to get information but also for the constituent to get information about what we know, what our position is.

Plus, we have issues outside of the policy part. We have issues of process and there is always the politics. It's important for us to be able to say, "Yes, I understand that's your point of view and let me explain what the politics of this are and why the process may not deliver the outcome you want."

It's easy to assume we don't know a lot about an issue, even though it's intricate. People tend to think members of Congress only look at what's going on in their committees. Or they think that because of a political position their party may take they may not be interested in discussing something. Or they think because of a vote you took in the past you might not be willing to be persuaded that things have changed or there is new information.

Lobbyists have gotten a pretty bad name lately; some deserve it, most don't. Lobbyists work for constituents—the same people I work for—they just do a different job.

These are people that are doing specific outreach to influence members of Congress, to educate members of Congress, to make sure the correct information is given to members of Congress—and to make sure the correct information comes back so that people understand there can be an accommodation or perhaps there has been a complete misunderstanding.

The most important thing for people to remember is that we work for you. I'd like to have a boss that appreciates me, that informs me what I need to do, that holds me accountable.

I get held accountable every two years on Election Day. It's the opportunity to re-hire me. I'm very aware that my constituents are running around with their hair on fire, taking care of their families, keeping their businesses going, dealing with elderly parents. Politics isn't on everybody's agenda.

But our democracy needs the care and feeding of its citizens. The most responsible way for people to be involved in their government is to be an educated voter, to participate in the political system by making sure they are influential in the process. That includes talking to the member of Congress and contributing to them financially if they think they are doing a good job.

People need to know that in this representative government, they have to take an active role.

Colin Grinnell

Colin Grinnell is Staff Director for the California Senate Governance and Finance Committee. Committee staff members are often referred to as "consultants."

As consultants, we are subject matter experts in specific policy areas. We serve members of the legislature and the public. When legislators, lobbyists, members of the public or anyone else wants to advance legislation in our policy area, it's our job to help them have a good understanding of the law, how it works, what the values are in that area of law.

Things like water, the environment, taxes . . . these things can be very intricate.

It's our job to know these areas well enough to communicate to decision makers and members of the public the legal context of a proposed change, what the consequences might be, the various benefits and drawbacks.

Our work product that is visible to the public is our committee analysis. These are public documents that we hope give a clear, concise explanation of a bill, the background and what the consequences might be.

Our work is seasonal. We start in December or January looking at the deadline for introducing bills, the schedule for committee hearings—for the senate that is generally middle to late March, for the assembly generally in June. That's when we have committee hearings. We publish the analysis for bills about six days before the hearing. There is a packet of analyses that come out for each hearing. You can pick it up in hard copy or get it online.

The good thing about the process is we have a good deal of independence to use our judgment to identify those issues in the analysis that need to be considered. As consultants we are administrative officers. We try to describe what is important about a bill. Members (senators and assembly members) can ask for an oral briefing or get any additional information they want. They make the final decisions on bills.

We work with the chairs of each committee; they are our first clients. We also work for all the members of the committee and all the members of the Senate as well as the public. If the phone rings and it's any of those, we help them out the best we can.

During session our analyses go out on Thursday morning before the next Wednesday hearing. We might have started working on an analysis months before. That might mean researching everything from court cases to academic research, calling practitioners, local officials or other experts. We try to gather as much information as we can and distill it into a document that's useful for the legislators. We answer inquiries from legislators or members of the public about specific issues. If a legislator is thinking about introducing a bill we might discuss it with them or their staff.

We handle administrative business of the committee, so on Wednesday morning we record all the actions of the committee, the votes, process the bills, make sure they get to the next committee. We draft amendments that the committee adds, so we need to be able to express in statutory language what is agreed to by the committee. Then we start on the next week's work.

It's a fun job. It's a wonderful opportunity and I get to work with amazing people. You get into this kind of work from a variety of places. I came to this job from a fellowship program where I worked with the local government committee for a year, then I went to work for a member of the legislature. In that job you learn the legislative process, how to make the world a better place in the way your boss wants to by analyzing the options.

Other consultants come from the private sector or state agencies where they have developed a special expertise such as water quality or recycling. You don't have to be a lawyer to be a consultant. It helps with some committees more than others.

Consultants have a unique entry point to solve problems. When legislators want to do something or a news report comes out about something, we are one of the first people to get a call.

Sometimes you have a chance to change the world. We did a lot of work over the last seven or eight years on the California Enterprise Program. When the political window opened the possibility of change and the Governor wanted to get rid of Enterprise Zones, we had done a great deal of analytical work that was picked up and it lead to eliminating Enterprise Zones and replacing them with something far superior.

That was incredibly satisfying. We've also done a lot of work on sales and use taxes, the Amazon issue. We worked on options that were enacted into law and became models for other states.

Sometimes change is very incremental. You fix 10 percent of a problem one year, 20 percent the next year. Sometimes for political or policy reasons you can't get everything that needs to be done at once. The economy today is very different from 10 years ago. Solutions for economic growth that were appropriate then may not be relevant today. The legislature turns over in membership every two years.

We work with many professional lobbyists. They tend to be incredibly smart people who represent folks to the legislature. They represent clients, some private or public entity. They have their own interests at heart and that's what they are paid to do. They are not compensated to advocate for the general public. Our job is to assess the case that the lobbyist is making. To get as much information as we can, to test the case they are making, find out if the information they provide is true. Is it complete?

Some lobbyists are wonderful to work with; some are awful. Some are trustworthy; some are not. They are a significant force in Sacramento. As consultants we try to be honest, forthright brokers of information. Lobbyists are members of the public like anyone else and have access here like anyone else.

Lobbyists can have a great deal of expertise that is valuable to us. Here on our committee we have two folks working on tax issues. That's 100 billion dollars in revenue, excise taxes, sales and use tax, corporation tax, property tax. It's impossible to know everything you need to know about those taxes, and lobbyists sometimes have information that helps us prepare material for the public and members of the legislature.

If, for example, we are talking about legislation regarding tax assessment you certainly want to talk to the assessors because that's what they do every day. They have very good professional lobbyists who represent them and provide information for them.

From time to time we get out in the state to see the effect of legislation. People can invite us, especially when the legislature is not in session and we are not always needed here in the capital. Getting out into the world and finding out the effect of legislation is a good thing.

With tax legislation we frequently have laws that sunset and you need to get out and see what's happening before you decide to reauthorize something.

If you have ideas for changes it's always a good idea to come in and get our sense for the viability of a proposal, for what the options might be, the hurdles you face, based on what we've seen.

If you are a member of an association such as the medical association or the Realtor association you can work through them. Sometimes the association is the best way, but sometimes the members are conflicted and the association can't find a consensus. You might contact your own senator or assembly member, talk to them, ask them to set up a meeting with a consultant working in the area you are interested in.

It's absolutely okay for grass roots advocates, non-lobbyists, to come see us. Our job is to be accessible to the public. A grass roots lobbyist is just like any other lobbyist. You can call us or email us and ask for a time to come in and talk with us. It could be anything from getting our advice or telling us what you are seeing in the policy area you are interested in.

Heather Scott

At the time of this interview, Heather Scott was chief of staff for Sen. Noreen Evans, who did not run for reelection in 2014. She has about 15 years working as staff for elected officials in Sacramento.

During session, it's easily a 10-12 hour day. We come in to work before the member (senator or assembly member) gets here, and often take an early meeting. The member comes in, we give a briefing about what's happening today, what she needs to know and do: You're presenting this bill, you're sitting in that committee, these are the problem children of the day. You're meeting with these people, here is the background on what they want to talk about. The member is getting handed off from staff person to staff person. I may be staffing these three issues; someone else is staffing different ones.

There's a lot of in-and-out, a lot of motion. Members have a lot to process in a very short time, so they have to put a lot of trust in staff. It behooves members to have staff who are more or less ideologically aligned.

Many times members have to be in two places at once, presenting a bill in one committee and voting in another, so we guide them back and forth, talking to them the whole time, telling them what happened when they weren't there, identifying people who are going to oppose the bill and the response. The consultants wanted something included. We accepted.

We schedule everything electronically. We keep three calendars moving. One is the member's calendar so we can see where she is supposed to be. Sometimes she'll call and ask, "Where am I supposed to be next?"

We have a staff calendar where everybody puts their meetings, so we can see who is meeting with whom. When somebody walks in the door we can get them to the right person and place.

I have my personal calendar with my meetings, doctor's appointments, anything else. I keep all three calendars on screen so I can see everything that's going on.

Drop-ins are the worst. People really need to make an appointment. It's just courteous. I don't want to tell anybody I can't meet with you. I want to hear people out, but if I have to go to committee, I have to go and then, I feel bad. If you want to talk with the right person about an issue, you really need to make an appointment.

If you want to lobby the governor, it's a hundred times harder. He's a busy man and represents an awful lot of people. I don't know if an individual could get to him. You would have to start with staff.

Former Sen. Joe Simitian used to run a contest called "There Ought to be a Law." He asked people to submit ideas. Over time, he got about 20 bills passed into law that resulted from constituent ideas. No lobbyist. No organization. Just a good idea. So it does happen.

A lobbyist is a person who works a very specific issue. I always take what they have to say with a grain of salt. It's their job to present their perspective. The job of a (staff) consultant is to be neutral and present all positions, to say these are the benefits, these are the liabilities.

A lobbyist is not neutral. What they say is weighted. If the lobbyist represents an interest that is along the same lines that my member generally thinks and feels, that means a lot. Lobbyists have a support staff to research issues and they represent some people experiencing problems, so in some ways they bring in very good information. Sen. Evans represents a wine-growing district. Wine growers have very good information about what is practical.

A constituent who comes in will generally not have in-depth knowledge about the opinion they are presenting. Often their positions are more emotionally-based, not fact-based. That's a broad generalization but it's sort of like the people who love guns versus the sheriffs who are dealing with a problem and know everything about guns. The opinions are valid and deserve to be heard, but information from constituents may not be as good, as well researched.

I enjoy the idea of public service.

A lot of garbage floats around here, but every now and again I get to play a part in something that is truly life-changing for people. There have been some really wonderful pieces of policy over the 15 years I've been here and I feel good that I've played a part in making that happen.

The most recent one was on the last night of session we passed a bill that will provide up to three days of sick pay for many low-income hourly workers who don't have any sick days. These are people who lose their jobs if they get sick or their child gets sick. We've all gone to work sick at some point in our lives and it's a miserable experience. Most places don't want you to come to work sick because you infect others. This legislation will be life-changing in a good way. Nobody should lose their job because they have a sick kid.

Probably 90 percent of the people who come to see the senator speak with staff. Professional lobbyists deal almost exclusively with staff unless they have their client with them who is a constituent. Staff are the first eyes on the analysis when a bill is coming up in committee. They are the ones making recommendations and summaries for the members. They are the first line of contact.

Members of the legislature have so much thrown at them and they operate on such a level of trust with their staff that staff becomes their eyes. If you are staff for a member who is on the public safety committee, you're dealing with the same lobbyists week after week because the same groups are interested in a category of bills. You might be dealing with the sheriffs, narcotics officers, the ACLU. They go back to the same staff person week after week. They usually don't even ask to talk to the member.

With the advent of term limits, there are not any legislators who have more experience than the staff. Committee staff is even more focused.

"Consultant" is the title we use for keepers of very specific information and knowledge of specific subjects. Committees are staffed by committee consultants, with the exception of public safety and judiciary committees, and those are all staff counsel. That's a very long-term gig for most folks and they become policy specialists. Some of them become even more specialized. On judiciary committee you have a consultant who deals with family law.

When something comes up on, say, foster care, all those bills go to that same consultant. They develop a very deep knowledge because they work with the same code section over and over and meet with a lot of the same players over and over. You get a very long-term perspective. They know how things used to be, what has been tried five years ago and the problems with that solution. They help channel the discussion and are very effective because they are not rebuilding the minutiae of an issue over and over again.

For the most part, on a public policy level, it would not be effective for volunteer advocates to work with consultants.

Most members (of the legislature) take meetings based on what committee they are chairing. So when Senator (Noreen) Evans was chair of the banking committee, she would meet with bankers. When Realtors were coming in during the mortgage crisis, she was dealing with them.

But staff can only take things so far. If you have a long line of opposition from established interests, staff will hit a wall at some point and you need the senator or representative to close the deal.

Everyone who gets elected and comes here wants to do something, to fix everything. I came here with that idea. I thought I could change the world. The best you can hope for is to modify it. Big change takes a long time. When Sen. Simitian first got elected, he introduced a bill to ban using cell phones while driving. He was mocked. He worked on that idea every single year he was here. It failed many times. He kept trying. Now that kind of law is ubiquitous around the country.

The longest I ever staffed a bill was five years, to get one bill through. But I finally did. It's exhausting. It's really hard on the ego. It's hard to pick up and keep going. Any big idea takes time and you have to take the beatings that come with it. Failure is part of the process.

Noreen Evans

Senator Noreen Evans represented California's Second Senatorial District, encompassing all or portions of the counties of Humboldt, Lake, Mendocino, Napa, Solano and Sonoma. She chose not to seek reelection in 2014.

I pay attention first of all to what my constituents say, second to what various associations say because they often include my constituents, and third I'll pay attention to others.

When I go in to vote, I have a binder. In that binder I have a segment related to each bill I'm going to vote on. It includes a list of all the contacts I've had from constituents, with a tally of the number for and against as well as selected comments from correspondence we've received. I get a stack of the complete pieces of written or email communications from my constituents on each issue I vote on. My staff works very hard to make sure that I know what my constituents are saying about every bill I'm voting on. My staff reads every email or piece of correspondence that comes in and many of those get forwarded to my attention. In addition to that I get a printout of non-constituent comments.

Time is very demanding at the capitol. I'm usually in a committee hearing, chairing a committee, or I'm on the floor in the Senate during session. If a person, or more often a group of people, has made the effort to come to the capitol, I try to spend at least five or ten minutes with them to hear their concerns.

People need to understand they won't always be able to call and get my personal time in the capitol. That's very difficult. Talking to my staff can be at least, as if not more, effective than talking to me. When you talk to a staff person, you are talking to an expert in the field you are concerned about. Let's say you are concerned about education funding. You will be meeting with someone who knows everything there is to know about education funding in California. If you meet with me, you meet with someone who has a general knowledge of these things, but not as specific as staff knows.

When a constituent meets with staff, that staff person is in charge of either getting back to them with an answer or helping them work through their problem with a state agency as an example. The staff person is going to do the actual work. That staff person will report back to me.

Generally I try not to say no. What I do try to do is tell people how they can find some alternative, source of funding or another answer to the problem they are trying to solve or how we might be able to change things in the future. Generally, I don't like to tell people no. That's a tough thing to have to say. For the most part we try to find solutions and if we can't find solutions now we try to figure them out for later.

Mark Leno

Mark Leno was elected to the California Senate in 2008. He currently represents the 11th Senate District of California, which includes San Francisco, Broadmoor, Colma, Daly City and portions of South San Francisco. Senator Leno chairs the Senate Budget and Fiscal Review Committee.

As the population of California approaches 40 million people and we have 40 senate districts, each California state senator represents nearly a million people. If just one tenth of one percent of those people contacts our office each week, that's a thousand contacts.

If you put it all together—the faxes, phone calls, emails and visits—we receive thousands of contacts each week when we are in session.

People who are my constituents, who live in my district, rise to the top. They are the people who elected me. That's who I serve.

When people come to me—lobbyist, citizen, anybody— I'm looking for a succinct, factual presentation of what the issue is. If you can't do it in 10 or 15 minutes, you're probably not well-prepared. There's nothing that can't be presented in that time frame. Whether you are speaking to me or one of my colleagues, to the degree that you are respectful of our time, the more welcome you will be.

When I get requests for "Can we just have 30 to 60 minutes of the senator's time" that person has no clue how limited our time is.

It's impossible for me to meet personally with everyone who would like to speak with me. People need to understand that when they are meeting with my staff, all their information will be conveyed to me. There is no need for concern if you can't meet with me directly.

When an issue is a really tough judgment call, it's not a 90-10, it's more a 51-41 call as to what's right, it helps me to know who is in support of a bill and who is opposing it. If a bill is supported by an organization that is aligned with the things that I've been fighting for, I'm going to pay great attention to that. With regard to how many constituents have phoned in or mailed in, that matters, too.

But that particular effect, how many constituents have made their voices heard, is a classic debate. Are we elected to mimic or parrot what we're hearing from our constituents? In that case, and I say this respectfully, we would be representing the voice of our constituents, yes. Or, are we there to lead? What does leadership mean?

Sometimes leadership means taking constituents to a place they don't even know they want to go. That's the tension of political decision-making. A good example is civil rights. I have colleagues who represent districts who don't support lesbian, gay, bi and transsexual rights. I ask my colleagues, "Are you just here to represent their prejudice and discrimination or are you here to lead them?"

People come in for many reasons. Oftentimes they don't really have an "ask." They just want to be heard. They've been harmed, they've been pained, they want some validation of what's gone wrong in their lives and why the state hasn't helped. Sometimes they don't understand the difference between state, local or federal government. They bring federal issues to our office. We have to explain there is nothing legally I can do, if, for example, it's an immigration issue. But we do our best to help them connect with someone who can help.

Sometimes they want to complain about a parking ticket and we try to get them to the right person.

Whether we are talking about business issues or other issues, the best I can do is welcome everyone to my office and make sure I have an open mind, that I hear everything they have to say and I am thoughtful in how I respond.

I have had any number of people say to me, "I'll support you in whatever you do going forward not because we agree but because you were respectful toward me when I was before your committee. You looked me in the eye, you paid attention to what I had to say." That's not always the case in committee hearings. My colleagues may be preoccupied with other things, looking at their phone, reading papers and they are not paying attention to what the person before them is saying. Maybe even in their own office they are abusive or dismissive. The best I can do is listen with intent and to be forthright about how I feel.

I'm not doing my job and I am providing a disservice to anyone who disagrees with me if I equivocate or am not direct about how I feel.

Back in my early days on the San Francisco Board of Supervisors, there was an issue about scientific experiments on animals at UCSF. I'm a big supporter of the University. I went into a committee hearing with one idea about the issue, and after hearing from people, my mind was changed. That happens a lot when you hear people out.

Sometimes people want to pressure me. I've had people from powerful corporate interests come into my office and close their argument with "You are going to be up for reelection. You're going to need our support." I'm confounded by this. It baffled me the first time I heard it. My first thought was, how dare you suggest that I'm going to redirect the way I think about an issue because of some political inference or veiled threat?

Sometimes it's innocent. Like all politicians, I have to raise money for my campaign and to help others in the Democratic caucus. In the situation I'm thinking of, I called a high-end donor and said you've made a contribution in the past and I hope you will again. The response was, "Oh I'm happy to give you a contribution." I said, "Thank you very much," and I was ready to move on to the next call when he said, "Oh, while I've got you on the phone, my son's going to be home from college this summer and I'm hoping he can get a position in your or some other office, can you help me out?"

That was innocent enough, but I had to say, Whoa. You just offered me a significant amount of money and now you are asking a favor. I don't think you want to be having this conversation as part of this phone call. I hope you understand. Let's talk again some other time.

Often the common wisdom about politicians is that we're all bought and sold, available for a price. In the case I just cited and others, I'm the victim. Someone wants to ask for something in the same conversation I'm asking for money. I have to slow them down and straighten them out.

Sometimes the reverse is true. We're talking about something policy-related and the person will say, "We'd like to help you with your next fundraiser." I have to say, "Stop. We're talking policy. We can't talk politics. Let's conclude our policy discussion and at some time in the future if you want to help me I'll be happy to talk with you, but we cannot do it in the same conversation."

I don't take it personally. It's often innocent, but it's wrong. It's disrespectful. Part of my job is to correct people when they get off track and talk about something that is either inappropriate or in fact illegal.

It can be subtle. A button that says "I vote." Any kind of threat is not well-received, whether from a corporate giant or a citizens' group suggesting, "If you're not with us, watch out." Threats are not appreciated and are not welcome.

There's a more artful way to make the point. A more appropriate way would be to say, "This is the way the 10 of us in your office feel and we are representing another 5,000 members in our organization and we feel very strongly about this." To suggest "or else" is where the disrespect comes in.

I'm sure there are some elected officials who will hear a threat and bend to it. I'm not that way. If I hear a threat, that pretty much ends the conversation.

I do listen to many lobbyists. It's a job. It's a career. Not unlike witches, there are good lobbyists and bad lobbyists. Sometimes I get very angry with them. They come to committee hearings and they lie. They stretch the truth. They deceive my colleagues. Once, in a hearing, the lobbyists brought in an expert with "Dr." in front of his name who told a powerful story that turned out to be made up. But those are the bad ones.

There are others that I may disagree with, but they are honest and play fair.

Marc Levine

Assembly Member Marc Levine was elected in November 2012 and again in 2014 to represent the 10th Assembly District, comprised of the communities of Sausalito, Tiburon, Larkspur, Mill Valley, Corte Madera, San Anselmo, Kentfield, San Rafael, Fairfax, Novato, West Marin, Petaluma, Cotati, Penngrove, Sonoma, Sebastopol, and parts of the City of Santa Rosa.

People from all walks of life come into my office. Just this week I've had everyone from chiropractors to high school agricultural students to doctors to accountants. When they are telling the story of how they work in the community and there's a specific piece of legislation that's going to impact them or impact our community, that gives me an incredible insight. It's a very meaningful exchange.

I'm very data-driven. I like to understand the broad impacts. But when there is a story that draws out what that data tells me, that's even more powerful. I don't rely solely on the data or even on an anecdote, but when the story matches the data, that allows me to understand and to explain how I vote on an issue in a succinct way. That's very important to me.

Right now we're dealing with how do we restore funding to education. The voters passed Prop 30, so we have much more revenue for education. Here in the North Bay, we have a wonderful agricultural heritage and we have funding for agricultural education in our schools. I had an opportunity to meet with high school kids who are farmers, raising hogs, cattle, even lizards. They were telling me what it takes to do this, what it means to have a business. These were high school students—incredibly sophisticated. They've learned a great deal. This was a very powerful way for them to convey the importance of sustained funding for those agricultural education programs in those communities.

I expect everyone who comes to me to ask for support for an issue. I like to be educated as to why I should weigh in. What are the intended outcomes? What are the possible unintended consequences that we need to understand before we pass a law?

Lobbyists come from all walks of life. They can represent nonprofits, environmental interests, business interests; they span a great range of issues. The end result of any conversation I have with a lobbyist is the same as the way I approach public policy generally: What is the problem we are trying to solve? How will this solution fix that problem without unintended consequences? I ask them to educate me on their issues and make the case for their side.

That's better than the lazy way that some lobbyists work. The lazy ones say, here are the groups that support this, here are the groups that oppose it. Rather than that, I want them to educate me.

If I understand the bill, perhaps I'll take a position. That works better for me than trying to legislate by who supports or opposes a bill.

We also are drawing districts differently, more independently, and I think that's going to cause legislators to think a little bit deeper, to understand issues better because we're going to be around to see what happens when we pass a bill and it becomes law. We'll have to live with the consequences. If it's not done right, we'll have to fix it, and that's difficult. So have to get public policy right. We can't be lazy.

In the past month I've had about 60 different meetings here in my district office and at the capitol. In every meeting there is someone who thinks their most important issue should be my most important issue, the issue that I should be championing. It's difficult to explain that there are 60 different "most important issues" that I need to wrestle with this month alone. There's only so much any one person can do and we all benefit when we focus on the core issues with which we can be most effective. It's a challenge.

If I can't really support you in the way you want, I might thank you for coming in and sharing information that you are passionate about. We might be talking about an issue that seems kind of silly, but it's important to that person, so it's important to treat it with concern. If we're genuine, if we are authentic, if we understand that constituent is coming in with the best of intentions, and that constituent hears that back from us, I hope they will have some peace and feel at least that they were heard. If we can't be helpful this time, perhaps we can in the future.

Should you keep trying to persuade me? Should you generate phone calls and emails? If you've tried to educate me, you've done your job. Anything more than that is essentially just spinning wheels. I'm not the type of politician that bends the way the wind is blowing. If I get bombarded with a whole lot of calls and I'm not learning anything new, if I'm not getting new data to help me change my position, it's not helpful.

I've had people who go beyond providing information and flood us with phone calls. They say if I don't respond in a certain way they will have to do something else and we take those threats seriously.

That happened this week. A member of the public who has visited my office and called my office on a daily basis said to one of my staff if I don't do X they will do Y. We escalated that to my chief of staff who told this person that they were not to speak to anyone except the chief of staff and we also alerted the sergeant at arms at the capitol.

The other kind of threat, that if I don't support you and your position on legislation, you won't support me. That is unethical and inappropriate, and there are avenues to report that to a committee that reviews ethics violations.

From the standpoint of someone threatening my re-election chances, in my first election we were outspent five to one in what was unfortunately a very negative campaign. Very few people survive an election where they are outspent five to one, but voters in Sonoma and Marin Counties rallied behind me. I have a great deal of confidence in voters. If that type of election were to occur again and someone was blisteringly negative against me, or spent a lot of money against me, I have a lot of confidence that the voters would do the right thing.

If someone makes a threat to retaliate if I don't vote with them, will that hurt their ability to communicate with me? Probably. It is unethical. If people choose not to support a candidate or donate to a candidate because of their record, that's fair. But if you couch a request for support of an issue with a threat of how you would act in an election, that goes beyond what is ethical or legal in California.

Money is an unfortunate reality in politics. People have to run a campaign. There's no public financing of elections, so we have to raise money for campaigns. People need to understand there should never be a connection between a donation and a public policy outcome. It has never happened to me that someone would mention a contribution in connection with trying to persuade me, and if it did it would be an opportunity to end the conversation and educate them as to why it's inappropriate to mention donations and public policy in the same conversation.

I like to learn something new every day. My staff knows that if they have information I can benefit from, I want to get my hands on it, learn from it. I can't do every meeting myself, but I can be briefed. I get a written report on most meetings that occur in the office. I get reports on community meetings, who was at the meeting, what was discussed, was there an ask for any action or follow-up from our office. That helps me understand what issues are rising in the district. I get reports on how many phone calls I get on specific issues. It's a little less data, but it helps me understand the inflow of calls and letters. Those calls that say simply vote yes or vote no get attention. We keep a record of every call and every email that comes in.

We deal with two very different sets of work. There are the policy matters we all work on. The Sacramento office tends to focus on those. Both the Sacramento office and the San Rafael office handle casework, but most of those calls come to the district office. Many of those can be resolved in a day or so.

My staff has an understanding of things that are time sensitive or important or things that are of a political sensitivity that I need to follow up with personally. Many of the most important calls we get are from people who have problems with unemployment benefits or health care benefits through Covered California or with DMV. The staff can usually resolve those.

I'm not sure if there is a difference in the impact between emails from our web site where we get their email address and their home address, or if they send an independent email or phone call or fax as long as we have a way to get back to them.

I have five people in the capitol office. They staff legislative committees. We have five in the district office and they work mostly on the casework. That's some of the most important work we do. When people call with a problem, we often are able to affect their lives very quickly by resolving an issue.

I'm here to serve everybody in the district regardless of their political party. We don't ask about that. Sometimes people will let us know, but it's not an issue.

Sometimes people come in and say, "Do you know X? Do you know Y?" And I say, tell me about it. I'm not in office to take a pop quiz. Educate me. I'm not an expert in many things.

When I go onto the floor of the house, I have a floor folder. It contains the bills I'll be voting on, a bill analysis, the list of letters I've received, sometimes the letters themselves about each bill.

Usually I take bills I'll be reviewing or perhaps some speaking material. It will be issue specific, about legislation that is before me. I have a folder for every bill that will come up. I have a bill analysis for each one.

Last week I had 500 letters put before me. I was already a co-author of the bill. This letter was more or less a form letter that 50 people had faxed or emailed into the office. The people felt that bringing in hard copies, a ream of letters, would push them over the top. They had a great deal of support for their issue already, but they wanted to make sure they did all their homework. As for impact, we were able to communicate with all those people going forward. I was already a supporter prior to receiving the form letters. This was more a measuring mark of their side doing everything they could do.

It's issue by issue. If the issue is important, if it resonates with me, if it warrants further introspection, the form letter may have no effect at all. It depends on the issue, not the letter.

I heard from one constituent that there was another constituent who had been trying to get a meeting with me. My staff wasn't aware of this. I picked up the phone and invited him to come to my office. We had a good meeting and I was glad I made that call.

If you want to be effective in meeting with a policy maker, you need to understand what your problem is and what is the solution you want. Is it good for you and for the broader public? If you can communicate that, you'll be very effective. Sometimes I have meetings in my office and it's almost interchangeable who the people are. They'll say we need more money and that's it. Anyone can say that. That's not enough. You need to explain why you need a certain amount of money and what that money will do. What effect will the money have?

Don't see the legislator as the only person you have to meet with. Staff can be your ally as well. I have tremendously talented staff. They are very thorough. They are able to vet issues and to help constituents present their issues better. I have a limited amount of time and staff is able to do the follow up work. Constituents should see staff as an ally.

Dustin Corcoran

Dustin Corcoran is Chief Executive Officer for the California Medical Association (CMA), a non-profit professional organization of over 39,000 physicians. At the time of this interview he was the association's Vice President of Government Relations, and thus chief lobbyist.

There are five lobbyists here at CMA in addition to myself, and a couple of contract lobbyists. It's not that legislators don't hear from us. They hear from us just about every day. But what's important is hearing directly from physicians, the person in the district who actually has to deal with the issues and the consequences of legislation passed here in Sacramento. They know that I'm paid to advocate on behalf of physicians and so to be able to hear from constituents directly is vitally important. In fact it carries more weight, often, because they know that somebody's taking time out of their very busy day to contact them and express an opinion on legislation.

It makes a tremendous difference if constituents have called about legislation. When I walk in the elected official is eager to listen to me. Say they've gotten ten phone calls from physicians in their district. That's critical because when I walk in, I'm telling them here's how you're going to be able to give a good answer to the physicians in your district. They are very

155

eager to write a letter back and say that they delivered on behalf of their constituents. So it makes the reception much more welcoming. When we walk in and it's not the first time they've heard about the issue. They know it's an issue that's important to their constituents back in the district.

What they want to hear from a practicing physician in their district is the effect legislation is going to have on their ability to be able to practice medicine. That's the key difference. Where we may come up as professional lobbyists and be able to wade through the minutia of legislation and talk about what's on page 7 of the bill, what they're looking for from constituents is an understanding of how its going to impact patients and the ability to deliver quality care in their district. Just a few bullet points is often enough to communicate to the legislator effectively. Very often they will hear from a constituent and then call and ask us for more information and more detail on what their constituent called about.

It makes our job as lobbyists easier here in Sacramento, when elected officials know they're going to vote with physicians or against physicians. They have to go back and explain that vote to somebody that they've met or somebody that they've seen face to face. Not to say that phone calls and letters aren't effective. But even more effective is developing a personal relationship with the legislators so they know that they're going to see you at the next community event or in some other context back in the district and have to look somebody in the face, somebody that they have a relationship with, and explain why they did what they did. It's much more comfortable for a legislator to be able to go back to that next community breakfast and tell a physician, "I took care of you on that bill" or, "I was able to deliver for you on that, I know that was a critical issue for you." Legislators always want to be able to deliver good news as opposed to bad news, and one of the strengths that physicians have, if they're willing to utilize it, is when we're battling insurance companies and some of the other folks that we often do battle with here in Sacramento, its very difficult for the insurance companies to be able to put a human face on the issue. They don't have a sympathetic face back in the district that's going to be seen at the next event. Physicians, when they do engage and get active, provide that human face that legislators going to have to see and interact with.

One of the biggest difficulties physicians have in advocating is that they are wealthy, particularly compared to what most legislators make and what their constituents make. Physicians, even the lower paid physicians, are always more highly paid than the average salary of those constituents outside of the medical community. Legislators themselves don't always make a lot of money. Physicians are expected to make money. It's widely perceived that's its okay and we want them to make money.

That's the common view held by most legislators. But at the same time to simply discuss pocketbook issues isn't always a winning strategy. A better way to handle it is to talk about the effect it's going to have on access to care and what it means for patients in the district. Are they going to be able to see a physician? Are they going to be able to see the best physician? Or are we going to create a two-tier system where those folks who may be on the lower end of the income spectrum are forced to seek care in an emergency department or some other venue that may not be the best? The way to handle that is refocus the issue on access to care and what it means for patients' ability to see a quality physician without having to directly discuss pocketbook issues.

Our President Elect was having a difficult time being re-enrolled as a Medi-Cal provider because he had moved offices — within the same office suite. He had been a Medi-Cal provider in good standing for a long time. But he had to go through a very laborious process to be able to continue to provide Medi-Cal to patients even though providers provide that service at a loss in this state. So we got him up here to testify in front of legislators and to personalize that story about what it means for physicians to go through this incredible bureaucracy to do the right thing in providing care to an underserved community. It showed how the state makes it even more difficult to provide care on top of the appallingly low reimbursement that the state pays. That awakened legislators to a problem they otherwise would have known nothing about. It was a backwater bureaucratic issue from a legislative point of view, yet that personalization of the story really brought it to the forefront in the legislator's minds and caused them to pass legislation to address that issue.

When telling your story, you need to think about what's going to impact the legislator, what's going to stick in their mind. If you can do something that really personalizes the issue, really crystallizes it, that shows what it means to not just you, but to the population at large and to the district. That has a massive impact. Because everything else might be equal, we might be able to counter the opposition in terms of how many lobbyists that they put up and how many resources they put up, to try and influence legislation here in Sacramento. But the key is if we can turn out physicians and have physicians provide those stories. That always puts us over the top. It's always a struggle to find physicians because they're very busy and have lives that are very much outside of the political spectrum. They need to remember how important legislation is to their ability to be able to continue to practice good medicine in the state. Failure to engage causes bad outcomes, and we're always here as staff, for CMA, fighting that, but when physicians engage we win. It's always a big help to have those personal stories from the district. Legislators do respond, they do pay attention, and they pay attention a lot more to us as professional staff when individual physicians are participating at the district level.

One of the best things to do is to give a tour of your offices to a legislator. You'd be amazed at how interested legislators are about the goings on of medicine. Most legislators don't have a background in medicine and don't have a lot of familiarity with the medical process. So being able to go, walk through an emergency room, to be able to go walk through a pediatric office or an oncologist's office or any specialty is fascinating. It provides you an opportunity in a short period of time to bond with the legislator. You'll be amazed that many legislators, after having done that, will call you directly to seek your advice and input on issues affecting medicine. Now you've now developed a direct line to that legislator. That's probably one of the most effective things that you can do, because then they not only understand you as an individual, but they understand the challenges facing your practice and have seen the place where you practice. Short of that it may be as easy as taking them to breakfast, or to a coffee, or showing up at one of their events. It's always a good way to establish a rapport with legislator. Their always looking for informed constituents to be able to bounce ideas off. Taking a little time out of your day and visiting with them means a lot to them.

Money is one of the most difficult issues to discuss because money and politics are inseparable. Politicians need money to be able to run for office. They're always under immense pressure to raise campaign funds and to be able to have those on hand, either for themselves or to help colleagues that may have a difficult race. It obviously has an impact on what we do here in Sacramento. To say that it doesn't have an impact would not be true, but it's not the only thing that drives politicians here in Sacramento. In fact most politicians came up here to try and do the right thing, to try and work on behalf of their constituents or on behalf of issues that they feel passionate about. That's not true for all politicians, but it's true for the vast majority who are here to try and do the right thing. To engage in the process, whether that's on the monetary side or just on the informational side is very helpful and very much appreciated by the legislator. Here at CMA, we have a PAC. We ask physicians to contribute to that PAC and we contribute to those legislators that are the most friendly to medicine. There's nothing like somebody in the district who has developed a relationship with the legislator hosting a little event, even if it's very small dollars for the legislator. It doesn't guarantee you anything; it doesn't buy you a vote. There are no quid pro quos in this. Anybody who tells you that's the case doesn't know what they're talking about. Votes are not for sale. You don't go around buying them. Probably one of the perceptions about lobbyists that is the most outrageous is that we go around doing that. I don't walk around with cash in my pockets or brown paper sacks. Those days are long gone. In fact campaign finance laws are very, very strict now, and influence peddling is a thing of another generation. So we have to be smarter in the way that we work as lobbyists and that's why grassroots is very important now, having physicians get involved.

Robert Naylor

Robert Naylor represented the San Francisco Bay Area's 20th Assembly District from 1978-1986, was Assembly Republican Leader from 1982-1984 and California Republican Party Chair from 1987-1989. He now works as a professional lobbyist representing various clients.

I got elected to the legislature because I'm interested in politics and public policy. When I left the legislature, I went back to practicing regular law. I was asked to take on a couple of lobbying projects and found that was my true love.

After politicians have been here in Sacramento for a year or two they realize that lobbyists are a valuable source of information. They get different points of view from lobbyists, pro and con. They view us as a useful part of the process.

From us they want good, accurate information. They want the ability to compromise, if necessary. They want somebody who can cut a deal among the interested parties if necessary so the opposition gets off their back. Lobbyists negotiate with each other; our clients negotiate with each other. When we can work out a compromise, the legislators are thankful that a deal was cut.

Grass roots contact from the district is very important. I have one group for example, the assisted living folks. Having owners of assisted living facilities that are in the legislators' districts talk to the legislators about legislation and what the impact will be, can be very helpful in swinging marginal votes.

People in the district bring the experience on the ground, the day-to-day experience of running a business, or, if you are a union member, the experience of working conditions. They bring the practical experience and language. It's not technical; it's not bill language. It's real people complaining about a real problem and needing a real solution.

For example, there's the requirement that an assisted living facility have insurance. It sounds very reasonable. But what happens if an insurance company settles one claim and then triples the premium? What happens to that small business if they can't afford the new premium?

That's the sort of thing you need to make some provision for in the legislation.

If you look at the subject matter of most legislation, it's not partisan, not Republican, not Democrat. Both Republicans and Democrats get bills passed. Partisanship comes into play with major philosophical issues like tax increases, lawsuit abuse— things like that. Most grassroots advocates don't have to worry about partisan identification. It doesn't come up. I've been in countless meetings with volunteer advocates, and having served in the legislature, I can't remember a time when party affiliation came up when talking about a piece of legislation.

The first question you get from staff if you want to bring somebody in is, "Do they live in my boss's district?"

Legislators want to talk with people from their district. You have an extra edge if you live in the district.

When you speak with a politician, the rules are very strict about discussing money. You can't talk about a campaign contribution in the context of making an ask or at a fundraiser.

Organizations that have political action committees and give money have a little easier time getting a meeting than people who don't. A lot of issues don't have moneyed interests involved. I represent the L.A. Transportation Authority and they cannot give money—it's illegal. I have no trouble getting meetings with legislators outside the L.A. area on transportation issues.

I won't say money has no influence, but it's exaggerated in the press coverage. Typically where there are moneyed interests, legislators are taking money from both sides, so I don't think it makes much difference in most instances. There are some legislators who are a little more interested in campaign contributions than others, but it's exaggerated, overall.

If a legislator doesn't seem to be with you or agree with you, I usually encourage people to find another way or find a compromise so you can make incremental progress toward what you are trying to accomplish. Legislators like to hear those kinds of proposals. Most of them don't like to say "No." They'll say, "Well, I'll think about it," or "I have this problem with your point of view." Showing support with letters from the district can help. Having a professional lobbyist take a read of the situation to see if you are wasting your time is useful. We deal with legislators all the time and we can tell if their feet are in concrete or there might be some flexibility.

There are some things people can't compromise on. A legislator from the East Bay is not going to be in favor of transporting Northern California water to Southern California. A legislator from Orange County is going to want to protect the beaches from oil drilling at all costs. Someone elected with overwhelming labor support is not going to vote against unions. But 90 percent of legislation isn't in that category. Some of it is technical. Some of it is just trying to make a law on the books work a little better. These are just problems looking for solutions and legislators are very open to solutions.

I advise volunteer advocates this way. Be brief. Have a four or five sentence maximum message you want to leave that gets to the crux. Don't be confrontational. Be reasonable. Emphasize that you are person dealing with a problem in your business or the community and you are looking for a solution.

There is power in numbers. The more members you can bring to bear, to a rally, to a lobby day—the better. Use the press, media and articles. That's all very helpful.

Lobby Days, when you bring a lot of people to the capital, are an expression of the intensity of concern. That gets people's attention, not just legislators, but their staff. They don't want to have these same people standing in their district office or raising a ruckus during an election. A good lobby day gives you credibility and clout. It induces the legislator and staff to want to help you solve your problem, if they can do it without offending a lot of people.

Elected officials have so many things they are trying to do at once, so many bills, too many committee hearings, too many meetings, so they rely on their staff to have some of the meetings. You should not be offended if you can't meet with the legislator, because on a given day that may not be practical.

You also need to think about committee staff. Committee consultants are very accessible and very important. They will be looking for ways to take the rough edges off legislation and satisfy concerns.

Bills are assigned to committees. The first important vote will be in a committee. Committee staff will analyze the bill. The first person you need to get to is the committee consultant who has been assigned that bill. They will include your point of view as part of the analysis of the bill. They sometime recommend amendments. The legislator who is sponsoring a bill pays attention to the analysis, as does the chair of the committee. So when you first get started the most important meeting you have is with the committee staff.

"Consultant" is the common term for committee staff. They are not outside consultants or anything. There's a chief consultant, an assistant consultant. Sometimes legislators call their staff "consultants."

If you are sponsoring legislation you need to start no later than right after the election. You have to find an author. That takes time. They are thinking about a lot of bills. You will have to approach a number of offices. It wouldn't hurt to talk with the appropriate committee consultant and show them a draft of your bill. The deadline to introduce a bill is the third week of February but you want to refine it before it's introduced.

Newspapers are not as important to the general public as they used to be because not as many people are reading newspapers. But legislators and their staff pay attention to what shows up in the press in their district in particular and in the *Sacramento Bee,* because everybody in Sacramento reads the *Bee* because it covers the capitol better than any other news outlet.

Al Statler

Al Sattler is a retired chemist who lives near Los Angeles. He is an active volunteer advocate for the Sierra Club.

I guess you could say I've been at this for a while, a few decades.

I remember going door-to-door with my father getting people to sign a petition. I don't remember what it was about, but I remember him shaking his head about how few people would sign it.

Then I was in college when the first Earth Day was held. To a certain extent, it's a matter of saying, "Well, I see we need to get something going to help protect the environment" and then pitching in to do something.

As for lobbying, one of the first times was with another volunteer who needed somebody who lived in the district to go talk to a member of Congress about a national forest issue, Steve Kuykendall, a Republican. I don't remember the outcome of our lobbying effort, whether he eventually supported our position, but I remember being pleasantly surprised at how polite and interested he was. I was hopeful.

More recently an issue specialist wanted me to go talk with a staffer who worked for a legislator. I was hoping the legislator would see our point of view and he turned out not

167

to. My suspicion is that it was because there is a major manufacturer in the district who was on the other side of our issue that he didn't want to anger.

I've gone to Sacramento for Sierra Club Lobby Day. Sierra Club staff makes appointments with legislators or their staff. We had cordial meetings with people, even those who opposed us. There was one staffer who was very much in favor of fracking and it was interesting to talk with him. He was definitely on top of the issue. We made a couple of points and he said, "You know, if that's the case, I just might change my mind." We were pretty sure, but told him we would check to make sure we had our facts right. We made notes for Sierra Club staff to follow up with him.

What legislators and their staff want from a volunteer like me, above all else, is accurate information. It helps to have more than one voice. I have a network of people in the district who care about environmental issues. When we have a hot issue I call or email them and ask them to make sure they contact the legislator. I send them background information.

When I'm concerned about a bill I go to LegInfo (http://www.leginfo.ca.gov) and find out as much as possible about the bill before I talk to anyone or send an email. One of the important resources at this Website is the analysis by legislative staff about the impacts of a bill and also a listing of who supports and opposes the bill.

Legislators tend to listen more to people who can vote for them. If you are not someone who can vote for them, they will typically pay much less heed to what you have to say. That's been my experience. When I talk to a legislator, I make sure I have some people with me who live and vote in the district.

It helps that I'm involved with the Sierra Club political committee here. We did the initial interview with the candidate about environmental issues and then endorsed him. The campaign was intense. I spent a few hours every weekend "walking, knocking and talking," as we called it. I got to know the campaign staff and volunteers very well.

The benefits were enormous. We managed to elect a candidate who was much more sympathetic to environmental issues, Assembly Member Al Muratsuchi. Then I was surprised to find that he hired some of his campaign staff to work in his office. We had gotten to know each other in the campaign and now I can pick up the phone and talk with them, ask what's going on with a bill. I don't do it too frequently. I don't want to be a pest, but I do it when I feel the need.

Elected officials frequently don't get many calls on issues. It's a little bit like the line from the song "Alice's Restaurant." If one person calls it has a small effect. If 10 people call then they really take notice. On the other hand, if you are speaking on behalf of a well-known, respected organization, that amplifies your voice a lot—especially if others in the district are delivering the same message.

Here are the lines from the song:

You know, if

One person, just one person does it they may think he's really sick and

They won't take him. And if two people, two people do it, in harmony,

They may think they're both faggots and they won't take either of them.

And three people do it, three, can you imagine, three people walking in

Singin' a bar of Alice's Restaurant and walking out. They may think it's an

Organization. And can you, can you imagine 50 people a day, I said

Fifty people a day walking in singing a bar of Alice's Restaurant and

Walking out. And friends they may think it's a movement.

Pat Libby

Pat Libby is Professor of Practice and Director of the Nonprofit Institute at University of San Diego. In that role she develops and teaches best practices for the management of nonprofit associations.

I encourage everyone who is starting an advocacy campaign to do a substantial amount of research on the issue and then boil that research down into a double-sided fact sheet. There's a lot that goes into producing that fact sheet. A lot of research, a lot of strategy about how to name and frame that issue, the coalition members that are listed. Sometimes you want to include examples of legislation from other states that mirror your legislation.

The fact sheet is important because it's a synthesis of all that research. It encapsulates what your campaign is about. It tells the story. It's a tool that the lobbyist or advocate can use to walk the legislator or the legislative aide through the main elements of that issue.

In addition to that very important piece of paper, you must have a web site. That's important to get people involved in your campaign. Use Facebook, Twitter, whatever works. But you also need to have paper to leave an artifact behind. When you are lobbying people they can take a look at your fact sheet and they can delve into it later.

The electronic age is a double-edged sword. I get so many things asking me to click on something I can't read them. We're all so busy we don't have time to click on everything. If I have a piece of paper in front of me I'm more apt to read it.

A lot of times boards of directors of nonprofits don't understand what the issues are, the issues that impede the nonprofit from being able to fulfill its mission. For example if there are many people that are served by a nonprofit that are encountering a problem time and again then that organization has a moral responsibility to do something to alleviate the problem. Those messages about the problem need to be clearly communicated to the board so they understand they need to take action.

Sometimes board members don't understand that nonprofits have the legal right to lobby. You have to educate them. All nonprofits, the minute they incorporate as a 501 (c) (3)—tax exempt under federal law—have the legal right to lobby. It's very simple to get started. Just fill out the IRS form called the 501 (H) election. Because of the (H), I call it the "Have At It, Have Fun, Go Lobby" form. It's a one-line form (plus the name and address of the organization). All you have to do is sign it.

People sometimes think exercising this option will lead to being audited. Study after study shows that doesn't happen. The other misperception is that your organization will have to do more accounting for your form 990. You'll actually less accounting to do because of the legal latitude the 501 (H) designation gives you.

It breaks my heart when I hear people in nonprofit organizations say they shouldn't get involved in politics, that politics is dirty. I like to explain to them that significant laws were passed because of nonprofits. My favorite is the

Americans With Disabilities Act. That law was passed in large part because of a man named Justin Dart and the nonprofit he formed to pass that legislation.

Before it passed, people in wheelchairs we often homebound. They couldn't attend a university or go to a movie or even go down the sidewalk to the bank. That law helped millions of people and it exists today because of the lobbying of nonprofit groups.

To any board member who is discouraged from advocacy by professional staff, I say, shame on any staff that is not willing to engage in nonprofit lobbying. You can feed people one at a time, but if you engage in advocacy you can feed many, many more.

If you are in the work of providing services, art performances or scientific research, whatever your mission, you can have much greater impact by lobbying.

The research indicates that only 2% of nonprofits lobby. My theory is that most people fell asleep during high school civics class. They are afraid because they don't know how the political process works. The analogy I use is that many people own pets, but they aren't veterinarians. You don't have to be a veterinarian to own a pet. You don't have to know all the intricacies of the legislative process to pass a law. You just have to understand the issue that is important to you.

For an organization, it starts with voter registration. You not only have to sit down with people and help them register, you have to tell them where the polling place is. You have to show them a sample ballot. You have to explain to them that they have a voice in government.

Elections are fantastic opportunities for nonprofits. Even though it is illegal for a nonprofit to endorse candidates, they can conduct a candidate debate. Think about it. If you are running a community based organization and you are able to turn out 2-300 people to listen to candidates debate issues, those candidates will look at the audience and say, "There are 300 voters. I need to listen to this organization."

In addition to that kind of activity, 501 (c) (3)s need to use all media: newspapers, TV, Facebook... even the old-fashioned copy machine is important. If you get an article in print, you can make copies of it and make sure the right people see it. Print is not dead yet. It still has an important use.

Online social media is very important for mobilizing people to action, to get them to call, to write and to otherwise contact their legislators. But print - newspapers - and TV are very important for raising the visibility your issue to the public and to legislators.

The most important thing, the most powerful thing you can do as a citizen advocate for your nonprofit, is meet directly with your legislator. Some people are disappointed that they only meet with the legislative aide rather than the actual legislator. Don't be disappointed. Those people are a proxy for the legislator. Staff and politicians are impressed if you take the time to go to their office, as long as you are calm, cool, collected and prepared.

No one likes to speak with someone who is angry or screaming, so don't go there. If you are prepared and have good materials, that is the highest form of advocacy and people will listen to you.

Your ability to generate a lot of emails or signatures on an electronic petition will have some impact, but only if you have tremendous scalability. If you can generate a million signatures, maybe. But the more personalized the communication, the stronger the impact. It's more effective if you get people to call or send a personalized letter, a personal message.

The more detailed you make your email, the better response you're going to get. I was recently surprised when I wrote to my congresswoman and my two federal senators regarding gun control legislation. I wrote a detailed email because it's an issue I feel passionately about. I got a call from one of the senator's offices and I got a detailed email response from the others. I think that's because I didn't just check a box and say I'm concerned about gun control.

I sent a very thoughtful, personalized message and I got a very thoughtful, personalized response. I was astonished that I got a phone call. What that said to me was even though this issue is in the press all the time, there aren't enough people picking up the phone or taking the time to write how they feel on these issues.

So don't be afraid. If your heart really is in service, lobbying is one of the most effective ways you can serve people.

PART III

The Tools

How You Gonna Call?

Members of Congress and state legislatures are buried in mail, phone calls, faxes, and email they will never see. They barely have enough staff to handle all the stuff that comes in, much less give it consideration. If you look at congressional websites, almost all instruct you to communicate only with your own elected official—the one you can vote for.

So focus on and multiply things we know have maximum impact. Personal, eyeball-to-eyeball relationships reinforced by thoughtful, permanent written communication are about the only things that can penetrate the tidal wave of messages flowing into politicians' offices. One chief of staff from a Washington office told me his Congresswoman sometimes meets with twenty people in a day. On top of all the other work members do, can you imagine how hard it is to remember any of this?

That's why your relationship with the politician and staff is probably the most important thing that will determine whether you get a response. If you doubt that, here is a list compiled by Bill Posey, who served in the Florida House of Representatives and then in the Florida Senate. Now he's in the U.S. House of Representatives. He's an effective legislator, willing to tell it like it is. He gave me this list when he was in the Florida House. The difference between part-time state legislators with small or no staff and members of Congress is evident.

U.S. Rep. Bill Posey's Effectiveness Rating Chart for Communicating With Elected Officials

100	Eyeball to eyeball. It's hard to say "no" when you're looking someone in the eye.
98	Personal letter (your own words, localized to the official's district with a hand-written note)
93	Thoughtful phone call with dialogue
80	Fax (personalized)
80	Meeting with senior staff
60	Email, if they know you
40	Phone call with instructions to vote "yes" or "no," leaving your name, which they may or may not recognize.
40	Meeting with junior staff
30	Obviously orchestrated impersonal communication in any form (gang phone calls from a convention, stimulated form telegrams, emails, faxes, etc., even with names of individuals in the district)
20	Email, if they don't know you
15	Preprinted anything (form letter, post card, issue paper, fax)
10	Petitions (no matter how many signatures)
0	Anything from outside the district, unless you represent a national or state organization with people in the district or are communicating to a committee chair or committee staff, in which case it could go as high as 80.

Bill Posey's Practical Pointers
for Grass Roots Lobbying

1 point minimum impact; 10 points maximum impact

1 point	Send photocopied letters
2 points	Send faxes on hot issues
3 points	Send copy of monthly magazine or newsletter
4 points	Call the legislative office
5 points	Send personal letters, regardless of quality
-2 points	Call them at their regular/real job about legislation
-5 points	Call them at home
-10 points	Call them at home late at night
-2 to 8 points	Publicize high ratings or awards depending upon quality and prestige

Meet personally by appointment to discuss positions and issues:

10 points	If you are a voter in the district
10 points more	If you are a contributor
10 points more	If you are both
1 point	If you supported their opponent and it was a nasty campaign (stay away until you are in a position to offer support next time)

When discussing business over dinner, use the opportunity to build relationships. Note that in most cases, $1,000 lobster dinners won't buy support for your issues, regardless of what the press says.

Author's note: I respect Bill and he has graciously appeared in several seminars with me and impressed the audiences with his forthrightness. However, I differ with him on one item. I think it is usually a waste of time to routinely send newsletters to politicians. Can you imagine how many people send monthly newsletters to politicians? They don't have time to read all the stuff they want to, much less your junk mail. They only need to hear from you when you have something specific to say. If you have something in a newsletter that merits attention, like a picture of the politician, send it with a letter, open to the right page with the item of interest circled in red ink.

Likewise, calling them at home. If the legislature is not in session, what else can you do? Most do not mind calls that use normal good manners.

Seven Steps for Creating a Powerful In-Person Encounter

When you visit an elected official, certain things will increase your effectiveness. This is a seven-step checklist for a successful meeting face-to-face with your elected official.

1. Tell him who you are: Not just your name and title, but a little about yourself, your personal history and your family. You want him to know you as a human being, not just an issue advocate. Make sure he knows you represent an organization, not just yourself, so he connects your visit to your professional lobbyist.

2. Provide an anecdote/story: Bring your issue to life in human terms. Tell about real people and situations from the politician's district who are or will be affected. Think "soap opera" with details, names, dates, and places; make it come alive.

3. Say what you want: Make sure the politician knows exactly what you came for: vote yes, vote no, cosponsor, speak to someone on the committee; be specific.

4. State why it's a good idea. Have at least three sound reasons why this elected official should support your position, especially focusing on the impact in the district.

5. Ask for support: Look directly in his eyes, lock on, and ask, "Will you vote with us (write the letter, cosponsor, or whatever)?"

6. Remember thank-you notes: Send handwritten notes to everyone you speak with.

7. Report results: Always detail the results of the meeting back to the headquarters of your organization.

Letters, Emails, Faxes: Make Them Work

The single most powerful weapon in your political arsenal is a letter on paper. That is more and more true in the age of email, Twitter, Facebook and YouTube. If you doubt me, Tweet your politician. Ask a question on their Facebook page. If it works, keep doing it. If not, use postal mail. Not just any letter, but a special sort of letter. Given the security measures in place for mail to Congress, your best bet is to print out your letter, put it in a large envelope and walk it to a district office. You can meet the staff and emphasize how strongly you feel about your issue.

Sending something that looks like an ordinary email will cause your communication to be discounted by many people in Congress and the legislature. So think about sending a PDF document that looks like letterhead and contains an ink-like signature. It may be printed and given to the member of Congress to carry outside the office, read on the plane, and so on. You can also use html to create an email that looks like letterhead.

However, many Congressional offices are wary of opening attachments, so email and faxes are a good option. Whatever you do, realize that appearances are part of the message and ordinary emails make less of an impression than something more businesslike. It is likely your message will be printed out and filed and read offline.

Yes, communication standards are changing. Yes many members of Congress (or their surrogates) respond to email. Do what works. However, if you want to increase your impact, try the ideas I'm laying out here. Do something to stand out of the crowd.

Considering all I've said about how elected officials want to hear from their constituents, I strongly recommend you indicate you are one up front. This means in the subject line of an email and the first line of an email, fax, or letter, you say something like "I live in District [XX]," giving the correct number for the district your official serves. For the U.S. Senate, "I live in [City] and [State]." If there is any way, make a personal connection. "You probably don't remember, but we shook hands at the barbecue last August in San Diego."

Why write? Letters on paper take more effort than a phone call and require you to get your thoughts in order. They are permanent. They can be copied. They go into files by issue. They are hard to ignore.

As you write, remember that, to be special, your letter must be thoughtful and personal. That is not to say that form letters don't have any impact. They do. When enough people send in letters saying essentially the same thing, using the same words, elected officials know they are part of an organized campaign. The fact that they know it's organized is not only okay—it's necessary. You need to be part of something larger than one person to get attention.

However, to truly change the mind or vote of an elected official, you need to appeal not only to their political instincts but also to their reason and emotion. They are interested in who is touched by your issue and how they are affected. How will it play out for their constituents? They are interested in who cares and how much you care and why you care. They are interested in whether you know what you are talking about and have anything worthwhile to say. Consider the following letter (name omitted).

This was given to me, rather proudly, by a nursing home administrator.

Read it and see what you think the politician's reaction would be.

Re: $29 million cut in Medicaid

Dear Governor,

Apparently, sir, you have forgotten that the elderly in today's nursing homes are those citizens who just a few years ago either fought, farmed, worked in industries, paid dearly for lost loved ones and paid taxes for World War I, II, Korea, and Vietnam. After the world wars, they paid for our hospitals, constructed universities, built interstates, fed other nations, and are directly responsible for all these contributions to the greatest nation that exists.

Today, after their strength has been spent and finances exhausted, they live hopelessly with their last days at the mercy of unappreciative politicians.

How can elected officials conscientiously live with themselves and their conscience, day after day spending billions after billions of American dollars for projects all over the world and failing to provide adequate funds for our own?

Cuts of $29 million, plus no increase in Medicaid rates for the care of the infirm elderly, are absolutely uncalled for. Governor, you can do better.

The next few months will tell whether or not you are a responsible person, the man who supports the health and welfare of the elderly, sick, and infirm, or just another heartless politician.

As a lifetime Democrat, I pray that you will come to your senses and act responsibly.

Sincerely,

John Doe

At first glance, many people like this letter. However, consider the tone.

What does this writer think about politicians—about the governor? What is the governor likely to remember from this letter? Would a staff person pass this on to the governor? If the governor did see this, I suspect the words "heartless politician" may hang heavy in his mind. I also suspect the governor does not see himself as a "heartless politician."

The only reason this letter gives him to change his mind is that one slightly upset person will think he's heartless. It is personal, but is it thoughtful? Would it cause the reader to stop and think? Would a reader have any reason to like the writer? A letter needs to convey respect, likeability and give specific reasons to support your position, just like an in-person meeting.

For example, what if the writer had said:

I'm writing to urge you to restore the $29 million in proposed Medicaid cuts. I realize you face tough choices in balancing the state budget. But I am worried that if the funds for Medicaid are cut further, the steps we will have to take to economize on the cost of care will be harmful to our elderly nursing home residents.

I've been an administrator for twenty-seven years. In my nursing home we are certified for 150 beds and usually they are all filled. The state pays us $88 a day to give near-hospital-level care to elderly residents. While we will always find ways to provide adequate care, if you cut the already meager funding we have, we will have to consider cutting some things that make a major difference in the quality of life our elderly enjoy. For example, under your proposed budget we have to consider cutting:

Trips to the mall for our mobile elderly. We take them once a week and for many it is their only contact with the outside world other than television.

Premium canned beans. We can cut back by using cheaper canned beans, but they have stems in them which often cause problems for elderly patients with dentures.

Staff. We have more aides on duty than the state requires because when an old person wants a drink of water, we want him or her to be able to get it promptly. At state minimums, an aide may care for ten residents and just can't get to them often enough.

There is more, and I invite you to come to our nursing home and see for yourself. We provide excellent care on the funds we receive, and in fact, nursing homes provide the most efficient and cost-effective care of any institutions in the state. But we are in danger of falling back to merely adequate custodial care because of rising expenses and reduced funding. The proposed budget cuts of $29 million in Medicaid will substantially reduce the quality of life for our elderly in nursing homes. I hope you will look carefully for other ways to balance the budget and restore the cuts as proposed by the Association of Nursing Homes.

Please let me know your feelings about this as soon as possible. If you want more information, I will be glad to provide it.

This version is designed to show sympathy for the governor, who has to make tough choices, and to give enough specifics to show the effect of budget cuts. The beans, the mall trip, the glass of water—all are designed to conjure up specific images. They are real examples given to me when I questioned nursing home administrators about what would happen if the Medicaid budget were cut.

Which letter do you think would have a more positive impact?

The second letter mentions the association, so the governor knows the letter is part of a widespread campaign. Notice that it also tells something of the experience and position of the writer. Remember, you are an expert in your area. It's important to let the elected official know you are knowledgeable.

Enough letters like this, thoughtful and personal, to governors and legislators or the resident and members of Congress, can have dramatic effect.

It helps if you let the recipient know you are politically savvy. When communicating with senators and representatives, state the number of their district and tell them you are a member of an association. Tell them:

- ✓ What you want.
- ✓ Where your issue is in the process
- ✓ When the next action step is likely
- ✓ What the effect is on real people

Keep it short. One page is enough. If you have more to say, put it in another letter and send it later. If you don't get a reply within ten days, call and ask what happened to your letter. You may have to send it again. Don't quit until you get an answer.

If you get an answer and don't like it, write again and ask for a conversation, saying this issue is really important to you. AND YET . . .

Over the years I have said, and almost everyone else in politics has said, a one-page letter is best. That's certainly true if you are trying to show that you, someone known and respected, is taking a stand. But I'm not sure that one page is best if you are trying to persuade someone to change his or her mind.

Remember the story about Texas State Rep. Patricia Gray who was meeting with some folks from her district, including me? As we talked, she noticed the name tag of a man with us and said, "You sent me a letter, didn't you?" She explained that she had not responded yet because she was still thinking about the issues raised in the letter.

In my mind, the fact she remembered it and was thinking about it was significant. She was chair of the Sunset Commission, which was reviewing laws to decide which should be retained, changed, or eliminated. I was so struck by the moment I got permission to reprint the following exchange of letters. First, the one to her:

The Honorable Patricia Gray
Texas House of Representatives
P.O. Box 2910
Austin, Texas 78769

Dear Representative Gray:

The Texas Credit Union Commission is going through the Sunset review process this session. There are various proposals to change the agency's governance and renewal term. I believe the proposals would be adverse to the agency's effectiveness because they emanate from the interests of banking groups.

The banking industry is engaged in an aggressive campaign to thwart the ongoing development and success of credit unions.

Please consider that the Credit Union Commission has been an effective regulatory body since 1969. It should be renewed for another twelve years — not for only four years as urged by banking interests. Also, the commission's structure of 6 industry members and 3 public members has worked effectively since 1983 when the public members were added. That structure should be kept intact because it has proven to be effective.

Finally, there is a proposal to complicate the Commission's existing administrative procedures with burdensome hearings for handling matters, such as charter and bylaw amendments. These matters have been effectively and fairly administered in the past. Such unnecessary hearings would unduly hamper the orderly development of credit unions.

Please give careful consideration to these matters. We want to be able to continue giving good service to our members.

Sincerely,

Roger McCrary

Chairman of the Board

This letter reads quickly, but it is a little longer than one page. It got the following response:

Dear Mr. McCrary,

Thank you for writing my office regarding your concerns for the Credit Union Commission. I am very supportive of the concept of credit unions and the invaluable service and access they provide to the community.

As you may know, on Tuesday, September 24, the Sunset Commission formally met to vote on the proposed recommendations affecting the structure of the Texas Credit Union Commission. The Sunset Commission voted to maintain the Credit Union Commission's autonomy; however, we recommended they comply with some public notice and comment before their hearings regarding approval or denial of charter applications, field membership expansion, and mergers.

The Sunset Commission also voted to improve the public's representation on the Credit Union Commission's Board, which is a policy that every state agency must comply with to ensure the public receives adequate input.

The Sunset Commission did not recommend consolidating the Credit Union Commission with the Finance Commission, since the Finance Commission will not be reviewed by the Sunset Commission for possible restructuring until 2001.

I am frankly at a loss to understand how these two very mild changes will undermine credit unions in Texas. I respectfully disagree that all is completely rosy with the regulation of credit unions. The Sunset review found that one-quarter of the state-regulated credit unions had financial problems serious enough to warrant a remedial monitoring program. Only twenty of those improved enough to be removed from remedial monitoring by the end of the year assessed.

Once again, I appreciate your taking the time to write my office regarding your thoughts on the Credit Union Commission.

Sincerely,

Patricia Gray

I like this exchange, even though the writer did not get what he wanted. Representative Gray gave careful consideration to his letter—she just disagreed. You can see in her letter that she had explored the issue carefully and had her facts in order.

Getting the politician to think is more than half the battle.

The other half is giving them something they will remember and that also comes from their district. Here is what I would consider to be an almost—as you will see—perfect letter. This letter resulted from a conversation I had with a physician who was coming to Washington with his professional association, The American College of Chest Physicians, Dr. Brendle Glomb, MD, PCCP, FAAP, in Austin TX. He hand delivered this to his two senators and representative's offices and discussed the letter with staff.

Senator/Congressman:

I am a Pediatric Pulmonologist and pediatric critical care specialist and a voter in Austin. I live and vote in your district. I would like to take the opportunity to illustrate a point about Medicaid and its devaluation of patient care, especially pediatric care.

The attached paperwork represents two invoices, if you will. (He actually provided copies.) One invoice is a recent bill for my automobile. Circled and starred is the price per hour of my Goodyear mechanics time to work on my car. The other invoice is an EOB (Explanation of Benefits; ("payment confirmation") from Medicaid for an hour of my time, spent with a 5-year-old boy with severe, persistent Asthma. Circled and starred is the price per hour that Medicaid decides my time is worth. The notations for that visit were 4 pages long and encompassed all aspects of the patient's interim and past pulmonary history, physical examination, family history, assessment and medical plans for his future.

My mechanic, a man or woman I don't know and have never met, was paid $84 per hour for his time (or his shop). I trust that he/she is properly trained and has the experience to do a good job. I have no idea. I was reimbursed $37.34 for the hour of my time. I spent 10 years in post-graduate training to become a specialist. I have been in practice for more than 15 years. I have an established and trusted relationship with my patient and his family.

The little boy, prior to seeing me, was hospitalized eleven times in the preceding 12 months. Three of those hospitalizations involved the pediatric intensive care unit and, on one admission, he was intubated and placed on a ventilator for 3 days. The number of emergency room visits was in the dozens per year. The cost to Medicaid for a year of this young boy's care ran in the tens of thousands of dollars per year. Since being cared for by a Pediatric Pulmonary specialist, 6 months ago, he has not been re-hospitalized, has visited the ER only once (for a broken arm), and sees me only quarterly, at similar or less expense to Medicaid per visit ($37.34).

A cost analysis, done by an outside consultant, shows that our average Medicaid reimbursement, per patient contact, is minus $10, i.e., it costs our practice $10 to see each and every Medicaid patient. There is NO REIMBURSEMENT. Essentially, we are taxed for the "privilege."

For the first time in my career, we have been forced to limit the Medicaid load that we can accept in our office, due exclusively to the cost of doing business. Unfortunately, we are the ONLY Pediatric Pulmonary group in Central Texas. Medicaid children will go without specialist care.

Thank you for your time and consideration in this matter. I am happy to speak with you at any time, at your convenience, about this and other healthcare issues related to both your Medicaid and private pay/insured constituents. I can be reached at the following numbers:

(He gave his home, office, cell and pager numbers.)

Sincerely,

Wm. Brendle Glomb, MD

So, great letter, right? What happened?

Nothing.

About two months later I called to follow up and Dr. Glomb was disappointed and discouraged. So I took another look at the letter and the situation.

1. He had talked to very junior staff at each stop on the hill. He wondered if they understood what he was talking about.

2. The salutation, "senator/representative," may have made the letter look like a form letter. It might have had more impact if he had addressed it personally to the senators and representative by name.

3. This may be most important: The letter doesn't make the ask. If offers to discuss, but does not say, I want to talk with you about this, when can we get together? It leaves the recipient free to do nothing. That's what happened.

4. Also, and maybe this is most important, there was no follow up, no request for response or action. Again, this leaves them free to do nothing.

My hunch was that this letter, good as it was, never got to a senior staff person or the members of Congress. After we talked, Dr. Glomb faxed another letter to the Congressman's chief of staff, by name, asking why nothing had happened.

He got a phone call and was told the office did not realize he wanted a response, and then he got a letter.

Here is the complete response over the Congressman's name and signature:

Dear Dr. Glomb:

Thank you for taking the time out of your schedule to come to Washington DC I was in a Ways and Means Subcommittee hearing during your visit and am sorry I could not meet you in person. As my health legislative Assistant Jacqueline Bender noted in her report to me about your March 6 meeting, I understand your concerns about the Sustainable Growth Rate (SGR) and the need to encourage more medical students to select pulmonary and critical care specialties. Your letter was particularly illustrative of the unsustainable effects the SGR will have on patients and physicians alike. I understand that this is particularly troublesome for those that you treat since you are the only pediatric lung specialist in Central Texas.

Based on your letter and your meeting with Ms. Bender, I was not aware that you were awaiting a reply. My office also did not receive the email you refer to in your facsimile. I do appreciate that you offered your expertise and assistance should I or Ms. Bender have additional questions.

As a member of the Health Subcommittee I will keep your concerns in mind as we work on a Medicare legislative package.

Please keep me advised of federal matters with which I may be of assistance.

Sincerely,

Lloyd Doggett

Notice that in this response, the writer had to re-state Dr. Glomb's position. This response letter had to be researched, written and approved by senior staff.

You Can Have Enormous Political Power

The system is outlined in this book. What I have described is nothing more than a compilation of tactics, techniques and strategies that work.

However, you must make a deliberate decision to use this system. I cannot promise you will win everything you want. You may, and you will probably suffer disappointment like Dr. Glomb. But I can promise if you do not get engaged, you will get nothing, and may have something taken away.

If you follow my suggestions, persist no matter what and keep a smile on your face, you will almost certainly win something.

ABOUT THE AUTHOR

Joel Blackwell worked fourteen years as a newspaper editor at the *Miami Herald* and *Charlotte Observer*. Tired of newspapers and hungry to find a way to participate in politics, he left journalism and set out to help organizations carry their political messages to the public, politicians, and press through consulting, keynote presentations, training sessions, and seminars. He ran for the state legislature in North Carolina and that experience taught him about the love affair between voters and politicians, which resulted in this book.

Known around the country as The Grass Roots Guy, he speaks each year to about fifty groups of ordinary people who come together in a state capital or Washington DC to lobby. He creates educational videos, DVDs and web content that helps people understand what actions they must take to influence political outcomes. After helping them understand how much power they can have, he often sits with them as they talk to members of Congress and state legislatures.

The information in this book derives from those sessions with politicians, as many as 150 a year. Joel uses his experience as a reporter to find what works and what doesn't, what politicians want from volunteer advocates and what they don't. He has interviewed more than five hundred elected officials—local, state, and federal—asking them what works and how they want to be influenced. He also conducted focus groups in nine states asking association members, corporate executives, and others why they don't write letters, make phone calls and give money to politicians.

From this experience, he compiled the tips and techniques in this book, which is designed to empower people to get what they want from state legislatures and the Congress.

You can find more information about the author on his website at JoelBlackwell.com. You can also reach him at 916.277.4884 or you can write to him via email at GrassRootsGuy@JoelBlackwell.com.

Index

19344895R00119

Made in the USA
San Bernardino, CA
23 February 2015